BestMasters

Mit „BestMasters“ zeichnet Springer die besten Masterarbeiten aus, die an renommierten Hochschulen in Deutschland, Österreich und der Schweiz entstanden sind. Die mit Höchstnote ausgezeichneten Arbeiten wurden durch Gutachter zur Veröffentlichung empfohlen und behandeln aktuelle Themen aus unterschiedlichen Fachgebieten der Naturwissenschaften, Psychologie, Technik und Wirtschaftswissenschaften. Die Reihe wendet sich an Praktiker und Wissenschaftler gleichermaßen und soll insbesondere auch Nachwuchswissenschaftlern Orientierung geben.

Springer awards “BestMasters” to the best master’s theses which have been completed at renowned Universities in Germany, Austria, and Switzerland. The studies received highest marks and were recommended for publication by supervisors. They address current issues from various fields of research in natural sciences, psychology, technology, and economics. The series addresses practitioners as well as scientists and, in particular, offers guidance for early stage researchers.

More information about this series at http://www.springer.com/series/13198

Larissa Katharina Senninger

Wisdom of the Crowd in Experiments

Springer Gabler

Larissa Katharina Senninger
Germering, Germany

ISSN 2625-3577 ISSN 2625-3615 (electronic)
BestMasters
ISBN 978-3-658-24293-0 ISBN 978-3-658-24294-7 (eBook)
https://doi.org/10.1007/978-3-658-24294-7

Library of Congress Control Number: 2018961139

Springer Gabler

This Springer Gabler imprint is published by the registered company Springer Fachmedien Wiesbaden GmbH part of Springer Nature
The registered company address is: Abraham-Lincoln-Str. 46, 65189 Wiesbaden, Germany

Table of Contents

List of Figures

List of Tables

Abstract

This paper analyses the phenomenon of wisdom of the crowd in experimental capital markets. Aiming to find out which market mechanism can aggregate different information in a meaningful way, a continuous double auction and a call auction mechanism are tested. The traded assets are glasses filled with different types of coins. Market participants receive different information about the value of the coins in the glasses. In line with expectations, markets with continuous double auction mechanism are better able to aggregate information and additionally take a shorter time. The deviation of market prices from the real values of the respective glasses in the continuous double auction is about half as big as the deviation in the call auction. Additionally, all participants were asked to give estimations about the real value of glasses before and after trading. This allows the analysis of the development of participants' beliefs after receiving different information and after trading. Receiving more information enables subjects to make better estimations, whereas more information improves the quality of estimations significantly only if it is a lot more information. Also, trading in a continuous double auction spreads more information among market participants in fewer rounds of trading compared to information distribution while trading in a call auction.

1 Introduction

In May 1968, the U.S. Submarine Scorpion disappeared from the North Atlantic. Even though the Navy knew where it was last located, it was unclear how far the submarine traveled since the last contact via radio. A range was estimated as the possible actual location of the submarine. But this search-radius was huge in diameter and in an area where the water was very deep. It was very unlikely for the submarine to be found by the search teams in near future, if they would have proceeded in the common way.

It was the Navy Officer John Craven, who had a very interesting and unorthodox idea how to conduct the search for the submarine. He constructed various scenarios what might have happened to the submarine and created a team that consisted of navy-experts from various fields, like mathematicians, submarine experts, geologists, etc. Instead of letting those experts discuss the possible scenarios in the team to find the location of the submarine, he asked every member for their individual guesses without them knowing what the other members of the team guessed. They were asked to give their opinion about the likelihood of the different events constructed by Craven and to estimate the location according to their individual belief.
The individual results of the estimations by the experts did not contribute much to finding the submarine. But Craven had another idea. He used Bayes' theorem of conditional probability to aggregate the individual estimates to an aggregated group-opinion about the loca-

L. K. Senninger, *Wisdom of the Crowd in Experiments*, BestMasters,
https://doi.org/10.1007/978-3-658-24294-7_1

tion of the submarine. And indeed, only five months later the submarine was found not far from the location predicted by the aggregated group estimation. (Source: Wikipedia, USS Scorpion)

Fascinating is that none of the individual estimates could predict the location of the submarine, not even close. Only the aggregation of individual opinions rendered a pretty good estimate of where the submarine was located.

This phenomenon is called “wisdom of the crowd” and will be a central issue of this master thesis and the experiment presented below. Wisdom of the crowd means that aggregating several independent and uncorrelated opinions or estimates renders a good estimate for the true value of the underlying (Surowiecki 2004).

There are different aggregation mechanisms used to aggregate information to observe the phenomenon of wisdom of the crowd. In my master thesis, I conduct a market experiment and determine the difference between call auction mechanism and double auction mechanism regarding their ability to aggregate information in an efficient way. I will focus on the question which of the two market mechanisms is better able to aggregate information so that ``wisdom of the crowd" works and market prices reflect the real value of the traded assets.

In **call auction (CALL)** markets participants are either buyers or seller and set prices and the respective quantity they want to trade once every period. After all bids and asks are made by all participants, all offers in the market are ranked and a market-closing price is set where supply equals demand. This price is the market price and there is only one market price each period.

In markets with **continuous double auction (CDA)** mechanism market participants can be buyers and sellers in every period and trade in continuous, mutual auctions. Market participants can set limit orders and market orders. All limit orders in the market can be seen by all other market participants and can instantaneously be accepted, so that a trade takes place. (Morone and Nuzzo 2016) Hence there can be many prices each period.

As wisdom of the crowd requires different and independent opinions (Surowiecki 2004), all market participants have different information. In my experiment participants receive different information about the traded asset in a hierarchic way. Information that can be ordered in a hierarchic way is characterized by the ability to be ordered according to the quality of information. This implies that it is obvious that information of one participant is strictly better and more helpful than information available to another participant.

The core question driving this experiment is to find an aggregation mechanism that aggregates different types of information in an efficient way. Additionally, the question whether more information is always better, or whether more information triggers ineffective behavior can be analyzed. This would be in line with the phenomenon of the J-Curve. (Schredelseker 1984) In group decisions when all team members are able to discuss in order to find an aggregated solution, all information of lower hierarchical status would be useless, but when analyzing wisdom of the crowd in capital markets, the phenomenon of the J-Curve could be visible.

The structure of this thesis is as follows. After an overview over the most important literature in each of the afore mentioned fields of research, I will present the results of the conducted market experiment about the efficiency of call auction markets and continuous double auction markets with respect to their ability to aggregate information effectively. First, the experiment settings will be described, followed by the results of the experiment. Both market mechanisms are tested in three sessions with a total of nine independent markets each. Therefore 6 experiment sessions with a total of 144 participants are conducted. Finally, I interpret the results and conclude the main findings of the experiment.

2 Literature

As there are several fields of research relevant for this thesis, I will start with literature on wisdom of the crowd in general and with literature on different types of information. Afterwards I summarize literature regarding call auction mechanisms and continuous double auction mechanisms and their respective ability to aggregate information efficiently.

Wisdom of the crowd means *"that individual knowledge can be extracted, while maximizing biases or misinformation by aggregating judgements"* (Makridakis and Winkler, 1983). If individuals are asked to estimate a specific outcome or give their estimation regarding a specific matter, several studies suggest that those individual opinions are biased in different ways. The forecasts might be too extreme due to overconfidence, might be anchored due to environmental surroundings, might be influenced by emotions, or might be under the influence of several other biases (Bettman et al. 1998, Gilovich et al. 2002). Clemen (1989) and Soll and Larrick (2009) suggest that combining individual forecasts leads to an efficient estimate of the true underlying value. Larrick et al. (2011) support this argumentation by the results of their study that show that the average of all collected opinions is a better forecast than the opinion of the average participant at their study. Additionally, Davis-Stober et al. (2014) find that the phenomenon of wisdom of the crowd is applicable to many different situations.
The first known relevant research in the field of wisdom of the crowd was conducted by Sir Francis Galton, a cousin of Charles Darwin, in

L. K. Senninger, *Wisdom of the Crowd in Experiments*, BestMasters,
https://doi.org/10.1007/978-3-658-24294-7_2

1907 at a cattle exhibition. He asked random people at that exhibition to estimate the weight of an ox. It turned out that the median of all estimates for the weight of the ox was 1,197 pounds and the true weight of the ox was 1,198 pounds (Galton, 1907). After that first contribution to the research about wisdom of the crowd, many others followed. Research in the form of experiments that analyze the phenomenon of wisdom of the crowd, but also studies of observations of this phenomenon in nature were published. A related phenomenon to wisdom of the crowd is ``collective swarm intelligence". It can be observed for birds, ants, fish, and many other animals. The idea is always the same: individually the abilities to estimate correctly are low, but the aggregate opinion of the crowd or swarm very often renders results that are close to the true value or optimal behavior.
Surowiecki (2004) analyzes the aggregation of individual information and argues that the aggregate opinion of a group is often better than the individual opinions would have been. The greatest advantage of using the phenomenon of wisdom of the crowd is that compared to consulting experts, the ``crowd's opinion" is much more objective and reliable. Additionally, the crowd's opinion might help to understand the specific behavior in different cultures. And finally, free markets show that wisdom of the crowd works without a central ``expert" opinion. Surowiecki (2004) also states some requirements for a wise crowd. Individuals not only need to have different opinions about the issue in question, they also need to be able to make independent guesses. Additionally, decentralization and an appropriate aggregation mechanism are necessary for a ``wise" outcome. Furthermore, Malone et al. (2009, p.17-18), focus on finding the *"different genes for collective intelligence, the conditions under which these genes are useful, and the constraints governing how they can*

be combined". They use systems like Google and Wikipedia to show how collective intelligence works and to demonstrate the advantages of using the crowd's opinion. They state that wisdom of the crowd works when *"resources and skills needed to perform an activity are distributed widely or reside in places that are not known in advance"* (Malone et al., 2009, p.15). Larrick et al. (2011) point out that the individual participants need to be properly incentivized to give their actual opinion to generate appropriate results. To guarantee a diversified crowd Herzog and Hertwig (2009) suggest mixing participants with different backgrounds, ask for their opinion independently, and maybe influence their original opinion by influencing them on purpose in one or the other way. A careful selection is necessary which information is shared with the participants and which is not. Lorenz et al. (2011, p. 9020) found that *"even mild social influence can undermine the wisdom of the crowd effect in simple estimation tasks"*.

Information that is distributed to participants is a difficult topic. Heminway (2014, p.827) raises concerns that *"information asymmetries among market participants can have negative effects on the markets in which information is used"*. On the other hand, different beliefs and information levels of participants are needed to observe the phenomenon of wisdom of the crowd (Surowiecki, 2004).

Huber and Kirchler (2003) and Huber et al. (2008) analyze the value of information for traders that are heterogeneously informed in a simulation and an experiment. They find that more information is not always better and may even lead to a worse performance in financial markets. That is unless it is much more information that is available to one investor in comparison to others. This effect is described as J-curve by Schredelseker (1984).

This is in line with Kirchler (2010). He finds that *"insiders outperform the market and uninformed computerized random traders perform equally well compared to average informed traders"*.

Copeland and Friedmann (1992) analyze the maket value of information by establishing a market experiment that allows participants to purchase additional information. They find that participants are willing to pay for information in more complex noisy environments, but under competition the price of information converges to a Nash Equilibrium where it is approximately zero.

In line with this finding Grossman (1976) states that *"if competitive prices reveal too much information, traders may not be able to earn a return on their investment in information"*. In his opinion it is only possible to sell information in a market when the market is noisy enough to hide the information that is introduced by informed traders into market prices.

In case a wise crowd can be established, their aggregated opinion is helpful in several ways. Budescu (2006) suggests that by aggregating different individual opinions the usefulness of available information can be maximized, impacts of extreme outliers can be minimized, and credibility and validity rise. In more recent literature about the phenomenon of wisdom of the crowd crowdfunding is the topic that dominates. A highly relevant study in this field is Mollick (2014). They analyze experts' opinions in times of new technological advances that allow new constructions like crowd funding etc. and in how far they agree with the crowd's willingness to fund. In the case of funding arts, they find that *"significant agreement between the funding decisions of crowds and experts"* (Mollick, 2014, p.1).

In cases where the opinion of the crowd and the experts diverge, they find a tendency of the crowd being willing to pay more than the experts might. They see a great opportunity in crowdfunding to use wisdom of the crowd to confirm experts' opinions and generally find that the crowd indeed tends to be "wise" in most cases. Martin (2012), Hakenes and Schlegel (2014), and Heminway (2014) also analyze wisdom of the crowd with the example of crowdfunding.

Martin (2012) argues that a common view is that crowds make awful decisions, as people are influenced by media and other influences. But he also states that if the wisdom of the crowd theory holds, this might have substantial potential for application to the crowdfunding model (Martin, 2012, p.28). The most important argument in his opinion is the combined purchasing power that the crowd has compared to individual investment experts and, additionally, the crowd represents not only investors, but also customers. The likelihood of a successful business can be deducted from the number of interested investors in the crowdfunding project.

Hakenes and Schlegel (2014) argue in a similar way that crowdfunding can be used as an aggregation mechanism for vague information as households do have tiny bits of private information about whether consumers will like the new product that is about to be financed or not. Crowdfunding shows how high the acceptance will be and thus the aggregated information of each individual household that is interested in financing aggregates to a pretty good picture of future success of a company.

Heminway (2014, p.827) states that the crowd in crowdfunding is rather heterogeneous. As investors often do not have a joint investment subject, and are geographically spreaded, crowdfunding is a relevant practical example for a wise crowd in reality.

Besides crowdfunding, there are several other fields of research that analyze the phenomenon of wise crowds.

Lee et al. (2011) analyzed the bids at the TV show "The Price is Right", where participants win if they guess the right price of the item in question. They combined all individual bids that were made for one item by all players and found that the aggregated bids were good estimates of the real value of the respective item.

Kittur et al. (2007) and Niederer et al. (2010) found Wikipedia as a kind of wisdom of the crowd application in real world that actually works.

According to Lichtendahl et al. (2013) to get a wise result from a crowd also the method of aggregating individual opinions is of high importance. Most studies use simple averages of individual opinions to aggregate those information to a group estimate (Larrick et al., 2011). Malone et al. (2009, p.17-18) compare mechanisms of aggregating information. They argue that averaging is a surprisingly good tool when estimating for example a certain number. But when it comes to more complex situations, especially situations that involve the exchange of money, more complex market mechanisms are needed to aggregate information efficiently. Budescu and Chen (2015) use a model that identifies experts in the crowd and weights the different opinions according to their relevance when aggregating the individual estimates to a group opinion.

Diamond (1981) analyzed *"a general equilibrium model of a competitive security market in which traders possess independent pieces of information about the return of a risky asset"*. He found that at the end of trading all information should be implemented in market prices.

This paper analyzes the ability of call market auctions and continuous double auction markets to aggregate different types of information to find an equilibrium that represents the estimation of the crowd. As participants in our experiment are also asked for their individual estimations prior to trading it is also possible to compare results from different market mechanisms to the simple average of individual guesses. In the following an overview over literature concerning both market mechanisms and especially the comparison between them is given. With respect to experimental asset markets Morone and Nuzzo (2016) give a good overview over the most relevant and leading research in this field of study. Asset markets in general are unique compared to other markets in the sense that prices have the role of reflecting available information in the market and that market participants can be buyers as well as sellers depending on their beliefs about the true value of the asset. (Sunder, 1995 and Plott, 2000)

A general requirement for prices to reflect information in an efficient way is to have a proper information aggregation mechanism. This can be a single auction mechanism as well as a continuous trading mechanism.

Leading research for the former type is Forsythe et al. (1982). They *"investigate a market where a generic asset with a risky payout is traded through a double auction institution"* (Morone and Nuzzo, 2016, p.3). They find that this market mechanism allows for an equilibrium to which prices converge over eight repetitions. This is in line with the results found by Smith (1962, 1964, 1976), Plott and Smith (1978), Ketcham et al. (1984), Holt et al. (1986), Davis and

Williams (1986), Gode and Sunder (1991), and Mestelman and Welland (1992).

Important for the experiment conducted in this paper is the research on different types of information being present in the market. There are four main information structures. First, there might be some market participants that have insider information and are fully informed about the true value of the traded asset. Plott and Sunder (1982) study how information can be transmitted from informed to uninformed market participants. Second, a market might consist of participants that are all only partially informed. Plott and Sunder (1988) argue that in such a setting it is highly dependent on the aggregation mechanism in the market and on the knowledge of preferences of other market participants whether prices converge to an equilibrium value. This argumentation is supported by Forsythe and Lundholm (1990) and O'Brien and Srivastava (1991b). Third, information gathering might be costly and thus market participants might have to weigh whether to buy additional information to make a better guess about the true value or not. Sunder (1992) and Grossman and Stiglitz (1980) investigate this setting and find that a model with information costs outperforms the previous mentioned models in informational and allocation efficiency. And finally, the fourth information structure possible is that information is received at a later point during trading, like Copeland and Friedman (1987) did in their study of a double auction asset market. Additionally, those four types of information can be mixed and subdivided into homogeneous information, so that every market participant receives the same information, or heterogeneous information, so that there is different information available for different market participants. Kirchler and Huber

(2007) show that different information available for market participants leads to fat tails and volatility clustering.

In the experiment presented in this paper, market participants will be provided with heterogeneous information that will be given to them simultaneously before trading begins.
Huber et al. (2008) present an experiment about whether there is a correlation between having more information and better performance. In this setting, the information was hierarchically ordered, so that it is possible to say that two participants have the same information, but one of them has an additional extra information on top. The contrary case would be that two participants both have different information and it is not possible to distinguish which information is qualitatively better. Morone (2008) finds that for high levels of information quality information aggregation occurs more efficiently.

To find the most effective mechanism to aggregate information is one of the central issues in experimental asset market models that aim to find an equilibrium price that clears the market (see Plott, 1982 and Ockenfels and Roth, 2002).

Continuous double auctions (CDA) and **call auctions (CALL)** are the most frequently analyzed market mechanisms in both theoretical and experimental works (Marone and Nuzzo, 2016, p.11-12). *"In a continuous double auction mechanism, each trader, at any moment during the trading period, is free to enter a bid (an offer to buy one unit of the asset for a specific amount of cash) or a request (an offer to sell one unit of the asset for a specific amount of cash). Submitted* *proposals appear on the book and become public information. Traders can also accept outstanding bids and asks, closing the transaction and making the relative price public information."* (Marone and Nuzzo, 2016, p.11-12) These are the reasons that make continuous double auctions so efficient in terms of trading opportunities and information distribution during trading across market participants. *"On the opposite extreme, in a single call market mechanism, each trader privately submits his purchase or sale order. For a single unit of the asset, the purchase order consists of the highest acceptable purchase price and the sale order represents the lowest acceptable sale price. When the trading period closes, the demand and supply scheme is derived and all the infra-marginal orders are executed at a unique price (clearing price), that is the intersection point of the demand and supply functions."* (Marone and Nuzzo, 2016, p.11-12) Compared to continuous double auctions call auctions only offer one trading opportunity per period. This reduces the number of possible strategies and information is distributed slower across market participants as information is only available after each trading period. There are also other variations of those two market mechanisms, like the uniform price double auction and the multiple call market (Cason and Friedman, 1996).

According to Marone and Nuzzo (2016), the most important contributions to call auction markets literature include Mendelson (1982), Ho et al. (1985), Satterthwaite and Williams (1993), and Rustichini et al. (1994). Double auctions are primarily discussed in Friedman (1984, 1991), Wilson (1987), Easley and Ledyard (1993), Glosten (1994).

In experimental research Cason and Friedman (1996) analyze four market mechanisms: continuous double auctions, uniform price double auctions, single call markets, and multiple call market. The efficiency of different trading mechanisms is calculated as the maximum profit that can be achieved through trading. They find that continuous double auctions and multiple call auction markets are more efficient than single or unique trading mechanisms. This allows for the conclusion that frequent trading opportunities in a period lead to higher efficiency of trading and therefore higher efficiency of the respective market mechanism. But on the other side, uniform price double auctions and single call auctions lead to higher information efficiency compared to continuous or multiple market mechanisms. In their study those market mechanisms showed less deviations of market prices from the equilibrium price that was predicted.

Smith et al. (1982), Friedman (1993a), Schnitzlein (1996), and Theissen (2000) focus on the comparison of continuous auction markets and single call auction markets. Smith et al. (1982) find a more time efficient price allocation for continuous double auction models and in most cases also a superior allocation efficiency for the latter models. Friedman (1993a) additionally finds a greater market volume for continuous double auctions compared to single call auctions. Schnitzlein (1996) on the other hand, finds that call auctions perform at least as good as continuous double auctions under asymmetric information and additionally, increase market liquidity and render less adverse selection costs. In a model with sequential information arrival Theissen (2000) found that call markets under-react to new upcoming information and continuous models where more efficient in this environment.

As most studies use call auction models and continuous double auction models to aggregate information, these models will also be used for the research conducted in this paper. Comparing a single period model to a continuous model not only analyzes the diverse effects of call versus double auction, but also the differences between a one period model and a continuous model regarding their ability to aggregate information.

There are also several empirical studies comparing those two trading mechanisms in a real world surrounding.
Amihud et al. (1997) and Kalay et al. (2002) analyze the Tel Aviv Stock Exchange, Kuo and Li (2011) the Taiwan Futures Exchange. Amihud et al. (1997) analyze the differences of trading under a call auction mechanism to trading continuously and find inefficiencies in call auction markets regarding the processing of new information in the market. They find a positive association between liquidity gains and price appreciation (Amihud et al., 1997). Kalay et al. (2002) find similar results and additionally state that large stocks gain more from the transformation of market mechanisms to a continuous auction than small stocks. The same change of market mechanism is analyzed by Kuo and Li (2011) for the Taiwan Futures Exchange. They found that spreads and volatility decreases with the introduction of continuous trading.
Empirical studies that focus on call auctions are for example Bacidore and Lipson (2001) and Barclay (2008) for the New York Stock Exchange and the Nasdaq, Smith (2007) and Pagano et al. (2013) also for the Nasdaq, Ellul et al. (2005) for the London Stock Exchange, and Chang et al. (2008) for the Singapore Exchange. They find higher price efficiency under call auction mechanisms.

Roll (1988) conducted an empirical study that focuses on price stability in instable times, like the 1987 crash. He finds that compared to continuous double auction markets call auction markets show much higher price stability in times of financial crises. Huber et al. (2014) found experimental evidence on varying uncertainty and skewness in laboratory double auction markets.

Based on the literature that exists on wisdom of the crowd, experimental asset markets, and information theories, the experiment in this thesis will compare continuous double auction markets with call auction markets. The comparison will be regarding the ability of different market mechanisms to aggregate information efficiently. Additionally, a simple average of individual guesses will be compared to each market mechanism. Participants receive different levels of information regarding the quality of information. The traded assets will be four glasses filled with different amounts of coins between 20 and 30 euros. The idea to use glasses filled with coins as assets is originally from Cain et al. (2005). Those assets allow for a precise definition of the asset and additionally allow to order the quality of information given to each participant according to the quality and usefulness.

In the following chapter the experimental set up will be described in more detail.

3 Market Experiment

3.1 Experimental Design

The laboratory experiment conducted in this paper aims to compare two different market mechanisms regarding their ability to aggregate information. Two treatments are applied, a call auction mechanism and a continuous double auction mechanism. The experiments are conducted at the Innsbruck EconLab of the Leopold-Franzens University of Innsbruck. The software used to encode the experiment is ztree (Fischbacher, 2007). For each treatment nine markets of eight participants each are conducted. As the Innsbruck EconLab has a capacity for up to 24 participants, six sessions are conducted in total, three markets per session and three sessions per treatment, where each row of eight participants is one market. This results in a total of 144 participants in both treatments, 72 each. Every round is conducted with new participants taking part to guarantee that the results are unbiased and participants have equal experience in the given setting.

In each market twelve periods of trading take place. Each of the twelve trading periods lasts three minutes. In the experiment participants are asked to trade glasses filled with coins. There are four glasses (A, B, C, D) of the same size filled with a different number of coins. The glasses contain one euro coins, 20 cent coins, five cent coins, and one cent coins. Each period each participant is endowed with five units of one glass and a certain euro amount. Not every participant is thereby endowed with the same amount of euros. More

L. K. Senninger, *Wisdom of the Crowd in Experiments*, BestMasters,
https://doi.org/10.1007/978-3-658-24294-7_3

detailed information about the initial endowment is given in subsection ``Endowment''. Every participant can either sell or buy those glasses to or from the other seven participants in the respective market. Before the experiment begins a practice period is conducted to ensure that participants understood the functionality of the respective trading system of the market.

Each glass is traded for three consecutive periods. Each participant starts each period again with five glasses and a specific euro amount. This means that profits or losses are reset after each period and participants restart each period with the same initial endowment. Before trading begins, participants are asked several questions to test whether they fully understand their task. Subsequently, a glass of the respective type is handed to the participants for examination. Thereby every participant can examine the glass for 15 seconds before he is asked to hand over the glass to the next participant. Subsequently the examined glass is traded for three periods. After three periods, another glass is given to the participants and again can be examined by each participant of the market for 15 seconds. The order in which the glasses are given to the participants can be seen in table 1.

Table 1: Order of Glasses across Rows and Periods.

Glass	Periods 1-3	Periods 4-6	Periods 7-9	Periods 10-12
Row 1	A	B	C	D
Row 2	B	C	D	A
Row 3	C	D	A	B
	D	A	B	C

After examining a glass and before trading starts, participants are asked on the computer to estimate the value of all coins contained in the glass they just saw. After they gave their estimation they see different information about the coins contained in the glass on their computer screens. There are four information levels (I0, I1, I2, I3). More detailed information about the distribution of information levels will be given in subsection "Information Levels". After participants received the different information about the coins in the glass, they are again asked to estimate the value of the glass.

Then the actual trading begins. Depending on the treatment participants either trade the glasses filled with coins in a call auction market or in a continuous double auction market. Also at the beginning of a trading period where no new glass is given to the participants they are again asked to estimate the value of the coins in the glass that they were just trading. This enables to see in how far the market price of the recent period influenced their estimation about the total value of the coins and in how far participants act in the market according to their estimations.

After three periods of trading each row receives a new glass with a different amount of coins and the same procedure is conducted again. Also after three periods the information level of each participant changes. Over all periods each participant traded each type of glass for three periods and had each information level for three periods. This implies that no one is ex ante better off or worse off over the whole experiment. Trading in each period is the same. Participants can each either sell glasses or buy glasses of the same type.

After a trading period is conducted, an overview of the number of glasses sold and bought, the participant's new amount of glasses and the new amount of euros after the experiment is shown. Every new period participants are again equipped with five glasses and the initial euro amount.

After all twelve periods of trading participants receive the amount of their final payment and are asked to fill out a general questionnaire about their person. More detailed information about the final payment will be given in the subsection “Payoff” and about the questionnaire in the subsection “Questionnaire”.

3.2 Individual Estimation

Asking participants for their individual estimations of the coin value in each of the four different glasses before trading begins, provides the possibility to compare the mean of all estimates to the resulting market prices. Additionally, it allows to quantify the usage of the different information levels that are given to the participants, as there is one estimation before anyone has received any information, one estimation after participants received the different information, and at the beginning of the second and third trading period. This allows to exactly observe the learning curve of the subjects. To incentivize appropriate estimations, participants earn additional money depending on how exact their estimations are. For each estimation that differs from the original value by less or equal to five percent a subject receives additional 20 cents, for each estimation that differs less or equal than 15 percent from the actual value, a subject receives additional ten cents, and for each estimation that differs less or equal to 25 percent the subject receives additional five cents. With this structure, it is possible to earn an additional amount of up to three euros with good estimations.

3.3 Endowment

At the beginning of each trading period each subject is endowed with five imaginary units filled with coins of the respective glass that is traded in this period. The endowment is shown on computer screen. Additionally, each subject receives a certain euro amount.
The glasses are of the same size and are filled with one euro coins, 20 cent coins, five cent coins, and one cent coins and differ in their overall amount according to the type of glass. Table 2 shows an overview of the coin distribution over the four glasses (A, B, C, D) and the respective glass value.

Table 2: Value of Glasses in Euros according to Coin Types Included and Number of Coins Included.

Coins	A	B	C	D	Total
1 Euro	9	10	7	6	32
	(9)	(10)	(7)	(6)	(32)
20 Cent	7.2	9.6	8.4	6.8	32
	(36)	(48)	(42)	(34)	(160)
5 Cent	7.05	9	7.6	8.35	32
	(141)	(180)	(152)	(167)	(640)
1 Cent	1.26	0.66	0.88	1.2	4
	(126)	(66)	(88)	(120)	(400)
Total	24.51	29.26	23.88	22.35	100
	(312)	(304)	(289)	(327)	(1232)

Figure 1: Glasses filled with Coins

Overall all four glasses together are worth 100 euros. Across all four glasses are combined 32 euros in one euro coins, 32 euros in 20 cent coins, 32 euro in five cent coins, and four euros in one cent coins. This makes a total of 100 euros distributed over four glasses. One glass is on average worth 25 euros. The respective glass values are all in a range of about 22 to 30 euros. Three of the glasses (A, C, and D) have rather similar values. This might bias participants. Still, as there is glass B with a rather high value compared to the other glasses, it is possible to test the ability of market mechanism to react to new information. Also, glasses have the same size so participants will anyway asume similar values. Figure 1 shows the glasses that were given to participants.

The euro amount given to subjects is between 194 and 316, varies from subject to subject, and can be seen in table 3. Overall each subject has an average euro endowment of 250 in every period. But to

keep the cash-asset-ratio on average at two, the average amounts had to vary due to the different values of the four glasses.
The following table shows subjects' euro endowment in each period depending on which glass they are trading in the respective period. In the last row we see that the cash-asset-ratio is constant over the whole experiment.

Table 3: Cash Distribution to Participants and Resulting Cash-Asset-Ratio.

Glass	A	B	C	D	Average
Subject 1	221	316	259	204	250
Subject 2	238	306	215	241	250
Subject 3	232	270	276	222	250
Subject 4	282	287	237	194	250
Subject 5	261	300	221	218	250
Subject 6	213	307	232	248	250
Subject 7	231	267	250	252	250
Subject 8	282	288	250	210	250
Cash-Asset-Ratio	1.9992	2.0002	1.9996	2.0011	2.0000

3.4 Information Levels

As mentioned before there are four information levels (I0, I1, I2, I3). This implies that participants in one market have heterogeneous information about the asset traded in the market. According to Surowiecki (2004) heterogeneous information is one of the most important requirements for wisdom of the crowd. Always two participants in each market receive the same information level about the coins for three consecutive periods of trading, so there are two participants in each market that have information level I0, two have I1, two have I2, and two have I3. Depending on the information level participants get information on the number and the amount of no type of coin, of one type of coin, of two types of coins, or on three types of coins. A participant with information level I0 does not get any information about any type of coins contained in the respective glass. A participant with information level I1 receives the information about the number and the value of the one euro coins contained in the glass. A participant with information level I2 receives the number and value of all one euro and 20 cent coins and a participant that gets information level I3 receives the number and value of all one euro coins, 20 cent coins, and five cent coins. No participant receives any information about the number or amount of one cent coins in the respective glass. Transferred to a real-world market situation this information structure represents different information that is available to market participants. One euro coins for example represent the major, prominent news that almost everybody sees in the news, i.e. news that almost can't be missed. An example is the VW-emissions-scandal. This information is available to almost all market participants and thus is almost instantaneously and completely integrated in the VW stock price. Information about the number of 20 cent coins represents information that is available, but is more difficult to get. This kind of information requires some deeper knowledge and more effort to get. Information on the internet can be taken for example. It is possible to get this information, but market participants need to invest time to get it. An example would be a balance sheet available on the company's website. And then there are the five cent coins. This information is only available to one quarter of the sample. This information is in real markets hard to get and costs time and sometimes money to gather this information. In this sample, no complete insiders are included as in real markets insider trading is forbidden. Therefore, no participant knows the number of one cent coins, thus this represents the noise that is not represented in market prices. The structure of information levels is summarized in table 4.

Table 4: Structure of Information Levels.

Information Level	1 Euro	20 Cent	5 Cent	1 Cent
I0				
I1	known			
I2	known	known		
I3	known	known	known	

Additionally, the distribution of information levels is designed in such a way that every participant receives every information level only once for three periods.

Only in three cases two subjects have the same information level at the same time for more than one time.

Table 5: Distribution of Information Levels among Participants over all Trading Periods.

Subject	1	2	3	4	5	6	7	8
Period 1-3	0	0	1	1	2	2	3	3
Period 4-6	1	2	2	3	3	0	1	0
Period 7-9	2	3	0	2	1	3	0	1
Period 10-12	3	1	3	0	0	1	2	2

3.5 Treatments

As most studies uses the single call auction model to aggregate information, this model will also be used in the research conducted in this paper. The other trading mechanism tested will be the continuous double auction mechanism, as it is used in many research papers and most real stock markets. Additionally, comparing a single period model to a continuous model not only analyzes the diverse effects of call versus double auction, but also the differences between a one-shot model and a continuous model regarding their ability to aggregate information.

The basic idea is to compare a market with a call auction mechanism with a market with a continuous double auction mechanism and determine which one is better suited to aggregate information efficiently.

Over the rounds of trading the fluctuation and volatility of the bid- and ask-prices for the coin glass are expected to converge to an equilibrium price that is close to the actual value of the coins contained in the glass, according to wisdom of the crowd.

3.5.1 Call Auction Mechanism

The first three sessions are conducted with a call auction market mechanism. In this market participants can in private post as many buy- or sell-orders as they want. Each offer is thereby for one glass of coins. Only if they submit their offers trading with other market participants takes place. Then the market builds an equilibrium price where demand equals supply and every trader sells as many glasses as he has sell-orders below the equilibrium price and every trader buys as many glasses as he has buy-orders above the equilibrium price. All transactions are conducted at the equilibrium price. Even if a trader would have paid more, he only has to pay the equilibrium price and also if a trader would have sold even at a lower price he still receives the equilibrium price. This implies that each trader sells as many glasses as he has posted at a price under the equilibrium price and each trader buys as many glasses as he has given buying orders at a price above the equilibrium price. Each trader can therefore act as buyer and seller in the market.

Figure 2 shows the used trading screen in ztree for a call auction market. At the top the respective information that a participant receives about the asset in this period is shown. Participants can insert buy offers in the box that says “Kaufgebote” by entering the price they are willing to pay for one asset. They can insert sell offers at the same time in the box that says “Verkaufsgebote” by entering the price they are willing to sell one unit of the asset for. On the right side the current euro amount available is shown on the right side as well as the number of glasses available. After inserting all offers participants submit their offers to the market by clicking "Gebote abschicken" on the bottom on the right side.

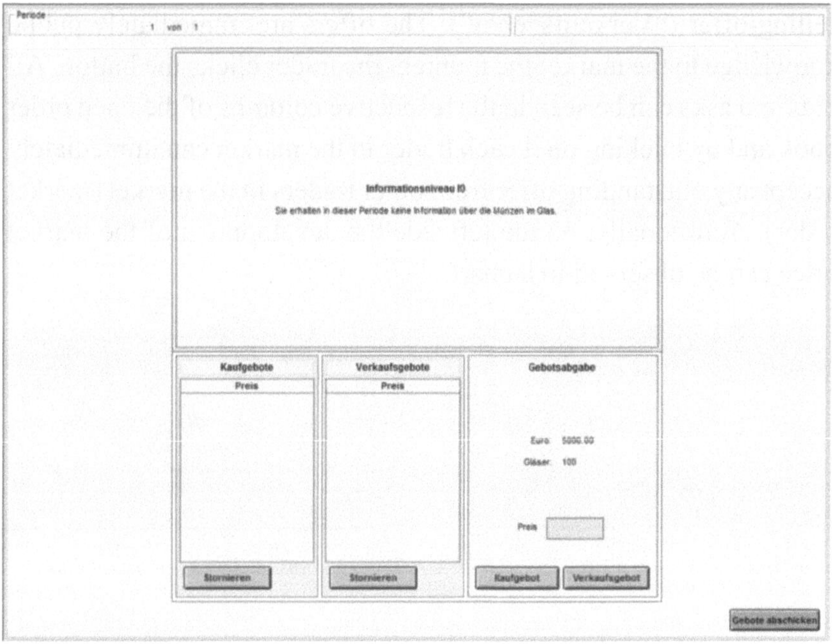

Figure 2: Trading Screen - Treatment CALL.

3.5.2 Continuous Double Auction Mechanism

In the continuous double auction market mechanism traders can also be buyers and sellers. Compared to the call auction mechanism the difference is that trading and matching of bids and asks takes place continuously over the trading period. Participants can make limit offers at which they would buy a glass of coins from other market participants or offers at which they would be willing to sell glasses to other participants. They do so by entering the price in the trading screen in figure 3, and either press buying-offer ("Kaufgebot") or selling-offer ("Verkaufsgebot"). The offers are immediately public knowledge to the market the moment the trader clicks the button. All bids and asks can be seen in the respective columns of the open order book and by clicking on it each trader in the market can immediately accept any outstanding offer from other traders in the market (market order). Additionally, on the left side the development of the market price can be observed in a chart.

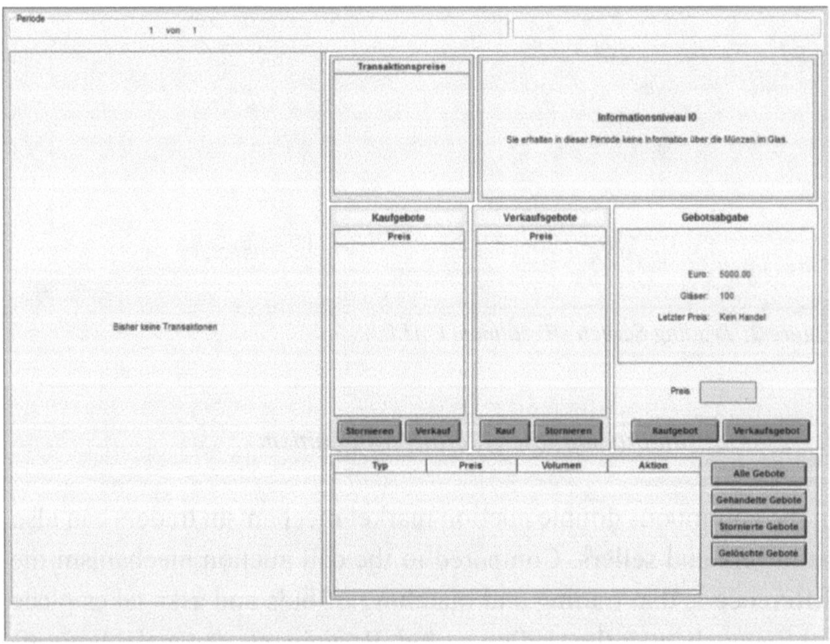

Figure 3: Trading Screen - Treatment CDA.

3.6 Payoff

To calculate the final payoff one of the twelve periods is randomly chosen. The payoff of participants in the respective period is calculated by the end-of-period euro amount that is left and the amount of all real glass-values that are in the possession of the respective participant at the end of the period. Those two amounts are added up and divided by 30. This amount together with the amount that has been achieved due to the estimations of up to three euros equals the final payoff.

3.7 Questionnaire

At the end a questionnaire is given to the participants to get some additional information like gender, age, and education. This provides the possibility to additionally test relationships between the trading behavior and some of the afore mentioned variables. In general, it allows to judge the representativeness of the group of participants and an estimation how well the findings of the experiment are applicable to real world markets.

4 Results

4.1 Estimations of Glass Value

To analyze several additional aspects despite the efficiency of the aggregation mechanisms participants are asked to estimate the value of each glass before and after information is distributed. The estimations after every round of trading allow to analyze the information distribution in a market in the respective trading mechanism through the interaction with other participants. But also, several other aspects can be analyzed with respect to the participants' estimations.

The first question is whether participants tend to rather underestimate or overestimate the value of the coins in the glass. This is analyzed four times - before any information is received, after participants receive information, and after the first and second trading round.

L. K. Senninger, *Wisdom of the Crowd in Experiments*, BestMasters,
https://doi.org/10.1007/978-3-658-24294-7_4

Table 6: Average Deviation of Estimations from True Glass Value.

Period	Glass A	Glass B	Glass C	Glass D	Overall
a	-11.86	-10.23	-10.80		-10.96
1	-3.58	-4.53	-4.49		-4.20
2	-5.53	-5.61	-5.10		-5.41
3	-5.03	-4.65	-4.57		-4.75
b		-11.08	-4.24	-5.50	-6.94
4		-4.30	-1.82	-3.48	-3.20
5		-4.79	-1.94	-3.25	-3.29
6		-4.74	-5.41	-3.24	-3.31
c	-5.94		-2.65	-3-32	-4.89
7	-2.78		-2.65	-2.39	-2.61
8	-3.40		-2.19	-2.63	-2.74
9	-2.80		-1.69	-2.69	-2.39
d	-5.15	-8.83		-2.72	-5.57
10	-1.84	-3.53		-2.87	-2.75
11	-2.45	-3.98		-1.63	-2.69
12	-2.55	-3.51		-1.52	-2.53

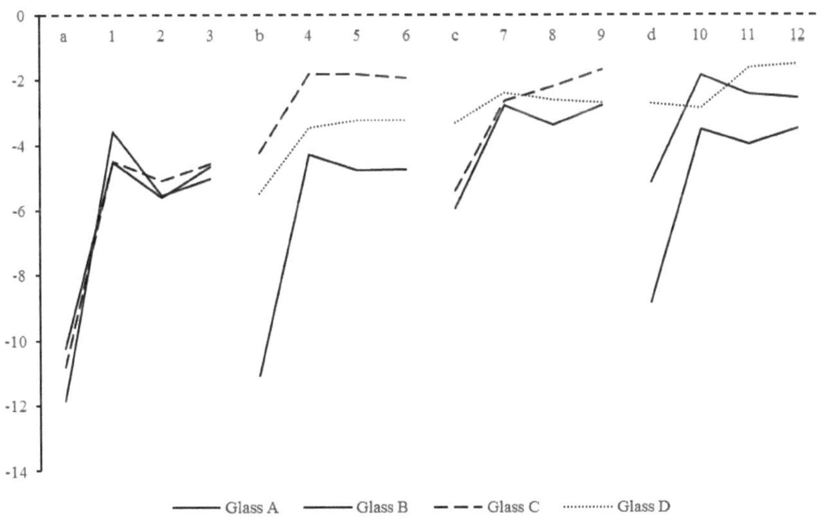

Figure 4: Underestimation and Overestimation of Value of Coins (in Euros) in the Glasses by Participants.

In figure 4 and table 6 in most cases the real glass value is underestimated by almost all participants. There is a general learning effect observable over all trading rounds. Therefore, it is important to look at each trading round separately. Additionally, it is also important to differentiate whether the trading period in question is the first one in general, or whether the trading period is the first one with a new glass, but there has been trading before. Subjects might be biased in subsequent rounds from information they received about other glasses and due to trading the glasses before. Also, they might have experienced a learning effect from trading the first glass. This is more than reasonable as the size of the glasses is the same and an anticipation by subjects that the value of the other glasses is similar having seen the development of the market price of the first glass is very likely. Before information is received participants prior to the first of the twelve trading rounds fail to estimate the value of glass A, glass B, and glass C, by on average -11.86 EUR, -10.23 EUR, and -10.80 EUR respectively (estimation a). Glass B was never traded in period one, see table 1. Looking at the results of estimations before receiving information about a new glass in period 4 validates that conjecture. Only Glass B that has an significantly higher value than the other glasses is still underestimated in the magnitude as before period 4 with a deviation of -11.08 EUR. The estimations for glass C and glass D are clearly influenced by the trading experiences in periods 1 to 3. Another explanation could be that the information distributed for the first glass traded still influences participants.

The learning effect can be seen by looking at the results for glass C and glass D in estimation b. They show an average deviation of -4.57 EUR and -5.50 EUR respectively. This implies that the estimations are two times as good as the very first ones although participants did not receive any information about the new glass at that point. Interestingly, the standard deviations in table 7 of the first and second uninformed estimation do not change significantly.

Table 7: Standard Deviation of Estimations from True Glass Value.

Period	Glass A	Glass B	Glass C	Glass D	Overall
a	5.81	11.99	9.88		9.23
1	4.53	8.44	5.16		6.04
2	5.41	6.08	8.08		6.52
3	4.35	6.83	7.26		6.15
b		5.86	8.72	11.18	8.59
4		4.48	5.61	8.69	6.26
5		4.47	4.61	6.95	5.34
6		4.37	4.40	6.37	5.05
c	4.76		5.43	4.43	4.87
7	2.98		3.30	3.18	3.16
8	3.18		3.49	2.79	3.15
9	2.89		2.91	2.67	2.83
d	4.48	4.02		4.50	4.33
10	2.30	3.63		3.42	3.12
11	2.88	3.62		3.13	3.21
12	3.40	3.44		3.17	3.34

While in the first estimation the standard deviations for the estimations of glass A, glass B, and glass C are 5.81, 11.99, and 9.88 respectively, in estimation b the respective standard deviations are 5.86, 8.72, and 11.18. This suggests that the estimations are on average more homogeneous for the first glass before any information is given, but is still spread similarly as in estimation a. Figure 5 shows that this changes over time.

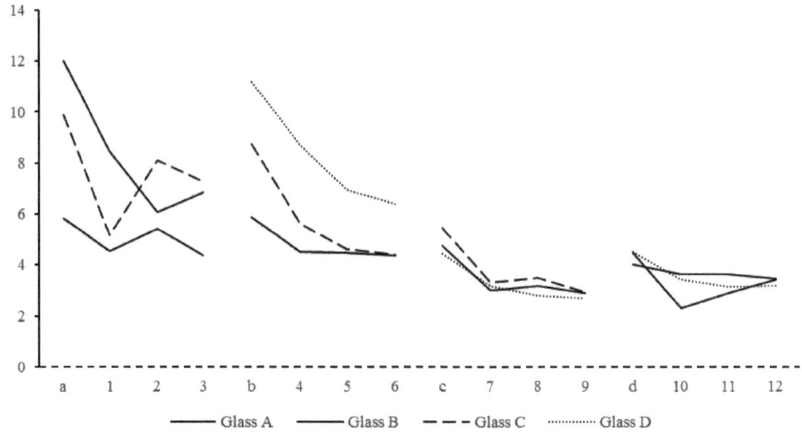

Figure 5: Standard Deviation of Estimations of Glass Value.

A clear tendency of the standard deviation is observable for the estimations of the four glasses. While the standard deviation in the first rounds ranges from almost 12 to about 6 depending on the glass that is estimated, this changes over the twelve trading rounds. Already in round 7 the standard deviation for all estimations is around 3 and stays constant at that level with minor deviations until period twelve. This suggests that a lot of information is disseminated through trading.

After the first observation of a clear tendency to underestimate the value of the glass at first sight, the estimation results after information is given to participants need to be analyzed. Especially with respect to the magnitude of the advantage through additional information. Figures 6 and 7 show the development of estimations of participants with different information levels. Figure 6 shows estimations before any information about the respective glass was received and figure 7 the development of informed estimations.

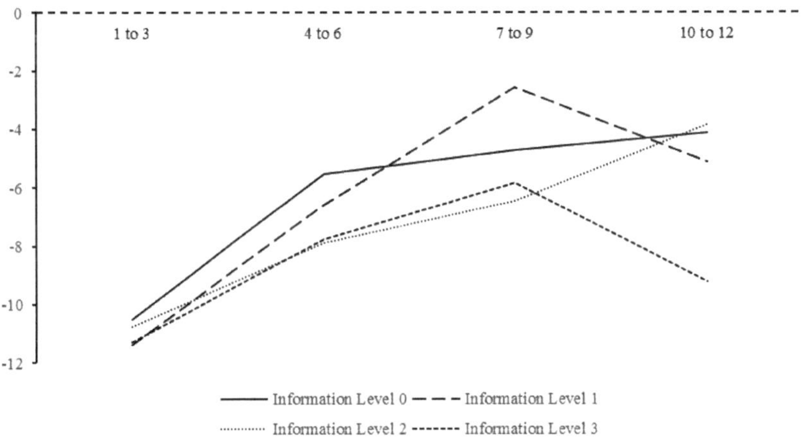

Figure 6: Estimation Results by Participants before Information about the Glass Value is Distributed.

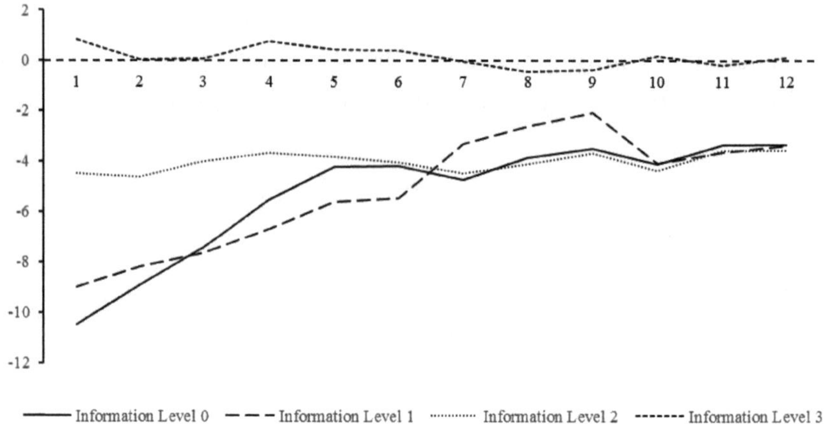

Figure 7: Estimation Results by Participants after Information about the Glass Value is Distributed and after every Trading Period.

Table 8: Estimations of Glass Value by Information Level.

Period	I0	I1	I2	I3	Overall
a	-10.49	-11.36	-10.73	-11.28	-10.96
1	-10.49	-8.99	-4.49	0.84	-4.20
2	-8.90	-8.18	-4.60	0.04	-5.41
3	-7.43	-7.64	-4.01	0.08	-4.75
b	-5.53	-6.57	-7.89	-7.77	-6.94
4	-5.53	-6.70	-3.66	0.76	-3.20
5	-4.21	-5.59	-3.79	0.44	-3.29
6	-4.17	-5.47	-4.01	0.42	-3.31
c	-4.71	-2.56	-6.46	-5.84	-4.89
7	-4.71	-3.32	-4.01	-0.03	-2.61
8	-3.86	-2.60	-4.47	-0.42	-2.74
9	-3.48	-4.06	-4.09	-0.35	-2.39
d	-4.12	-5.11	-3.83	-9.22	-5.57
10	-4.12	-4.06	-3.67	0.18	-2.75
11	-3.35	-3.64	-4.35	-0.18	-2.69
12	-3.32	-3.37	-3.57	0.13	-2.53
Average without Information	-6.21	-6.40	-7.23	-8.53	-7.09
Average with Information	-5.21	-5.13	-4.02	0.16	-3.55
Difference / Improvement	+1.00	+1.27	+3.21	+8.37	+3.54

In figure 6 the general tendency seems to be improvement of estimations. Although those estimations are made before any information is distributed this tendency seems to be a learning effect from previous rounds and similar glass values. Participants that receive I3, the best-informed level of information only in the last period have a worse performance than participants that already had I3 before. This might be since at that time they do not have the information and as they are I3 in the last three periods, they were worse informed before. This might explain the bad estimation prior to trading.

In figure 7 it can be clearly seen that the estimations improve over time and that the best informed, I3, also makes the best estimations, as expected. Additionally, the estimations get closer to the real value after trading. This can be observed in each of the three trading periods where one glass is traded. It indicates that the market mechanisms succeed in distributing information that is in the market. Interestingly, I0 is only in the first two periods significantly worse than the others, afterwards I0, I1, and I2 have rather similar estimation deviations, only I3 is strictly better over the whole-time horizon. Especially in the last three periods only participants with I3 estimate significantly better than participants with other information levels. For participants with I0, I1, and I2 it does not seem to matter which information they possess, the deviation of estimations is almost identical. This might be partly since each of those participants already had I3 for another glass before and therefore have a rather good impression what the glass might be worth.

4.2 Estimations in Call Auction Markets and Continuous Doublc Auction Markets

In this context, the question arises whether call auction or double auction are better in giving information to market participants. In figure 8 the development of estimations is illustrated for estimations by participants that traded with a continuous double auction. Figure 9 shows the same development for estimations made by participants that traded in a call auction.

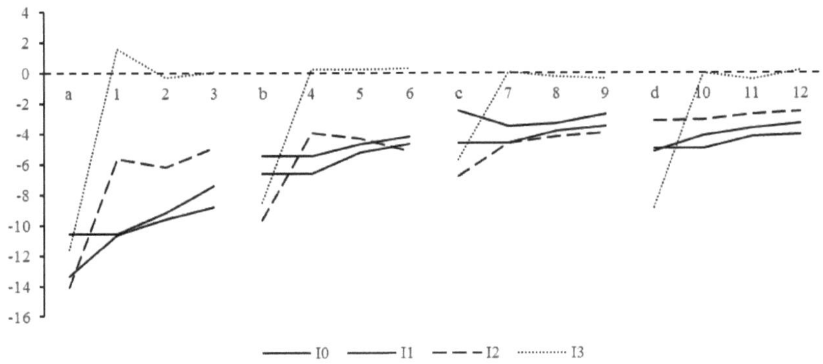

Figure 8: Estimation Results by Participants - Treatment CALL.

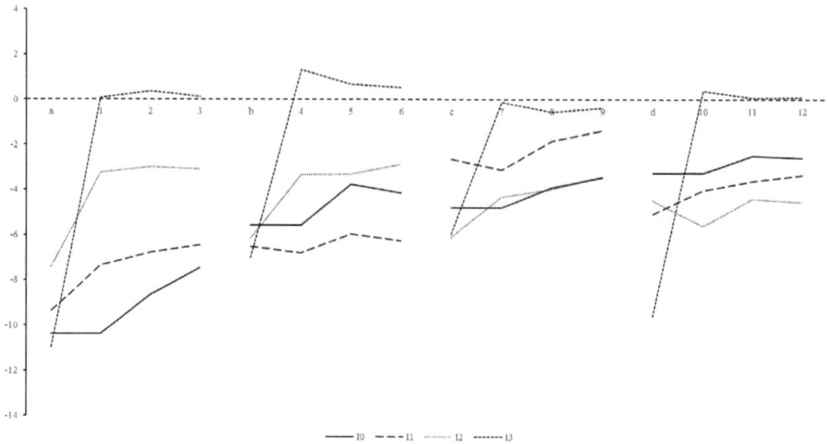

Figure 9: Estimation Results by Participants - Treatment CDA.

Table 9: Estimations of Glass Value of Treatment Group CDA by Information Level.

Period	I0	I1	I2	I3	Overall
a	-10.39	-9.35	-7.40	-10.95	-9.52
1	-10.39	-7.35	-3.23	0.09	-5.22
2	-8.64	-6.78	-2.99	0.37	-4.51
3	-7.45	-6.46	-3.08	0.13	-4.21
b	-5.58	-6.52	-6.14	-7.03	-6.32
4	-5.58	-6.81	-3.33	1.32	-3.60
5	-3.75	-5.96	-3.29	0.67	-3.08
6	-4.14	-6.27	-2.87	0.53	-3.19
c	-4.79	-2.65	-6.10	-5.96	-4.87
7	-4.79	-3.11	-4.31	-0.12	-3.08
8	-3.89	-1.85	-3.97	-0.56	-2.57
9	-3.44	-1.36	-3.40	-0.36	-2.14
d	-3.25	-5.06	-4.46	-9.60	-5.59
10	-3.25	-4.02	-5.59	0.39	-3.12
11	-2.49	-3.61	-4.40	0.08	-2.60
12	-2.60	-3.36	-4.54	0.10	-2.60

Table 10: Estimations of Glass Value of Treatment Group CALL by Information Level.

Period	I0	I1	I2	I3	Overall
a	-10.59	-13.36	-14.06	-11.61	-12.40
1	-10.59	-10.62	-5.68	1.59	-6.33
2	-9.17	-9.59	-6.20	-0.29	-6.31
3	-7.41	-8.83	-4.94	0.04	-5.29
b	-5.48	-6.62	-9.64	-8.51	-7.56
4	-5.48	-6.60	-3.98	0.21	-3.96
5	-4.66	-5.22	-4.30	0.21	-3.49
6	-4.20	-4.66	-5.16	0.31	-3.43
c	-4.62	-2.48	-6.83	-5.72	-4.91
7	-4.62	-3.53	-4.62	0.05	-3.18
8	-3.82	-3.35	-4.20	-0.27	-2.91
9	-3.53	-2.76	-3.95	-0.35	-2.64
d	-4.98	-5.16	-3.19	-8.84	-5.55
10	-4.98	-4.11	-3.12	-0.03	-3.06
11	-4.21	-3.68	-2.74	-0.45	-2.77
12	-4.05	-3.37	-2.55	0.15	-2.46

In figure 8 and in figure 9 enormous jumps can be seen after the information is distributed. As expected those jumps are the strongest for I3, then I2, then I1, and no jump for I0, as no information is distributed. Over the twelve trading periods those jumps get smaller in both market mechanisms. This indicates that both market mechanisms seem to have the ability to distribute information effectively. Also during the trading periods where one glass is traded minor improvements are observable in the estimations of participants of both types of market mechanisms. Figure 10 shows the direct comparison of estimations made by participants of the call auction and estimations made by participants of the continuous double auction.

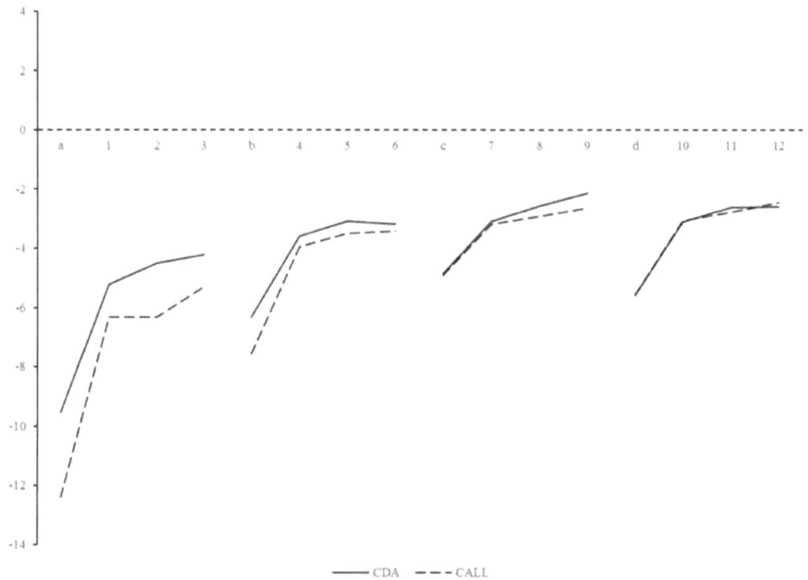

Figure 10: Estimation Results by Participants - Comparison of Participants of Treatment CALL and Participants of Treatment CDA.

On average participants of the continuous double auction estimated the value of the glass slightly better than participants that traded in the call auction. Interestingly this already starts at estimation a, before trading even started. This indicates that there might be just a general factor that participants of the first session just estimated better in general than those of the second session. To test the factors that influence how precise estimations are, a regression analysis is conducted.

$$Deviation\ of\ Estimation = \propto + \beta_{IL} * IL_i + \beta_{Gender} * Gender_i + \beta_{Age} * Age_i + \beta_{Period} * Period_i$$

$$DoE = Estimation_{ij} - True\ Value_{ij}$$

Deviation of estimations (DoE) is measured as the absolute deviation of estimations from the real value of the coins. The tested influencing factors are the respective information level of participant i, gender of participant i, age, and period in which the estimation took place. The influence of information level is high and with every additional information the deviation of estimation decreases by 1.74. There is also a difference between men and women. Estimations of men tend to be by 1.12 closer to the real value than the estimations of women. Age has no big influence, still there is a small tendency that the older people are, the better are the estimations. And finally, the period has an influence. With each period, later the estimations are on average by 0.4 closer to the real value.

Table 11: Regression Statistics - Influencing Factors for Estimations.

Multiple R	0.55
R Square	0.30
Adjusted R Square	0.30
Standard Error	3.75
Observations	1728

Table 12: Regression Analysis - Influencing Factors for Estimations.

	Coefficients	Standard Error	T Stat	p-value
Intercept	10.31	0.74	14.02	0.00
Information Level	-1.74	0.08	-21.49	0.00
Gender	1.12	0.18	6.15	0.00
Age	-0.05	0.03	-1.71	0.09
Period	-0.40	0.03	-15.37	0.00

4.3 Market Mechanisms

In the previous chapter, we saw that estimations of participants get better after trading. This implies that they gained valuable information during trading. In the following the prices in continuous double auctions and call auctions are compared and analyzed. Figures 11 and 12 show the price development for each treatment.

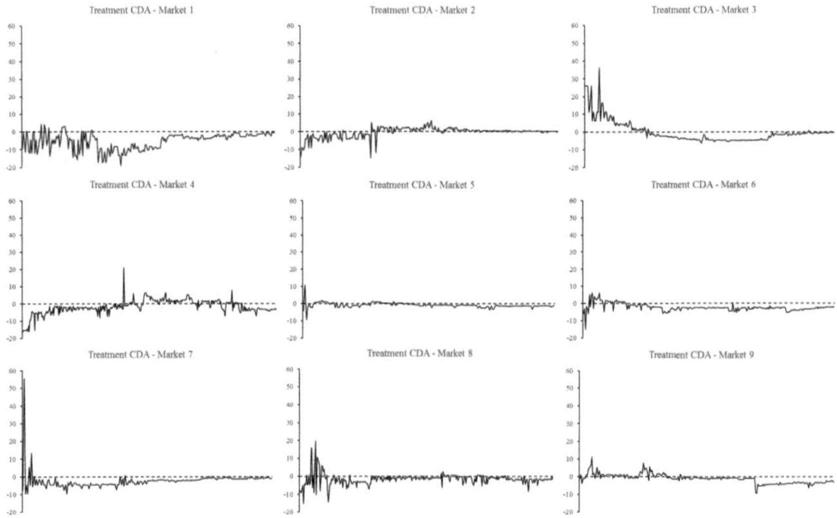

Figure 11: Development of Deviation of Market Prices from Real Value - Treatment CDA.

Figure 11 shows the market price development in all continuous double auction markets over twelve trading periods. It is observable that while the deviation of market prices is very high and volatile in the first trading periods, the market price converges in almost all markets very close to the real value, i.e. the deviation of market prices converges to zero.

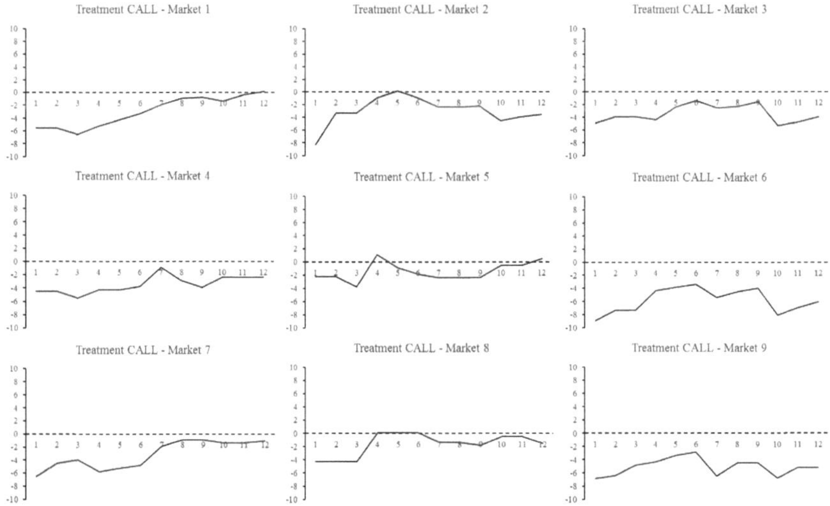

Figure 12: Development of Deviation of Market Prices from Real Value - Treatment CALL.

Figure 12 shows that a similar development is observable for call auctions. Still in this treatment the deviation of market prices from the real value converge to zero, but only in two of nine markets there is actually zero deviation at the end of trading. In all other markets market prices never fully capture the true value of the underlying. This implies that continuous double auctions are better able to distribute information equally among market participants. To be better able to compare the price development of continuous double auctions to call auctions, Figure 13 and Figure 14 show the development of end of period deviations of prices from true values in continuous double auction markets and end of period equilibrium prices in call auction markets.

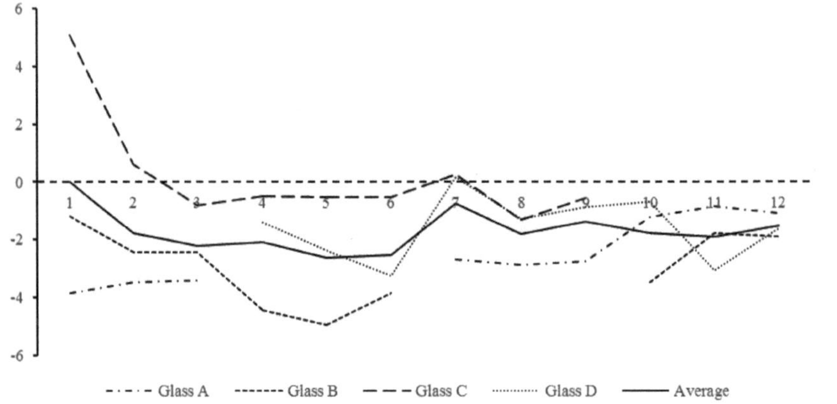

Figure 13: End of Period Market Prices - Treatment CDA.

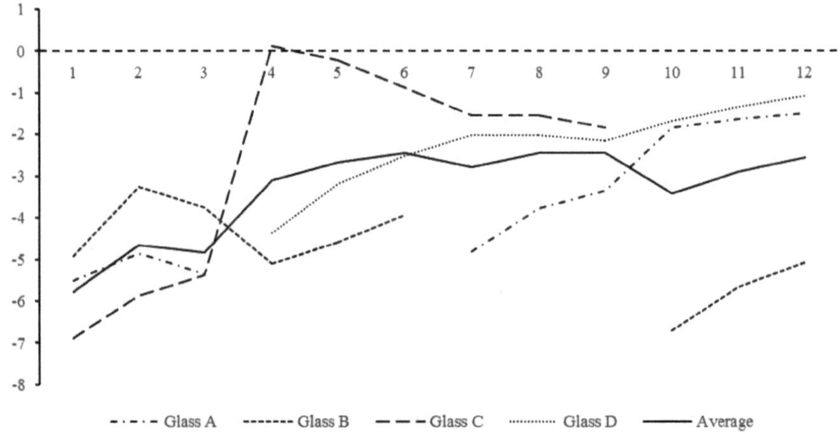

Figure 14: Equilibrium Prices - Treatment CALL.

In figure 13 we see that the deviation of market prices of the different glasses converges to about -2 over the 12 trading periods in the continuous double auction for all glasses. Figure 14 also shows a convergence to about -1.5 for two glasses, but still has an average deviation of -5 in period 12 for glass B. This might be since the value of glass B is much higher than the value of the other glasses. In continuous double auction markets, also the market price of glass B converged to about -2. This implies that continuous double auction markets seem to be more flexible in new situations, while call auction markets seem to react much slower, but not generally worse. Tables 12 and 13 show the average deviation of market prices from the real value of the glasses for continuous double auction and call auction respectively.

Table 13: Average Deviation of Market Prices - Treatmet CDA.

Period	Glass A	Glass B	Glass C	Glass D	Overall
1	-3.84	-1.18	5.09		3.37
2	-3.48	-2.43	0.62		2.17
3	-3.41	-2.43	-0.81		2.22
4		-4.43	-0.48	-1.38	2.10
5		-4.94	-0.51	-2.38	2.61
6		-3.84	-0.51	-3.23	2.53
7	-2.68		0.25	0.18	1.04
8	-2.88		-1.30	-1.26	1.81
9	-2.75		-0.54	-0.85	1.38
10	-1.21	-3.46		-0.67	1.78
11	-0.84	-1.76		-3.06	1.89
12	-1.08	-1.91		-1.61	1.53
Average	-2.46	-2.93	0.20	-1.59	

Table 14: Average Deviation of Market Prices - Treatment CALL.

Period	Glass A	Glass B	Glass C	Glass D	Overall
1	-5.51	-4.93	-6.88		5.77
2	-4.84	-3.26	-5.86		4.66
3	-5.35	-3.76	-5.36		4.82
4		-5.09	0.12	-4.35	2.61
5		-4.59	-0.21	-3.18	2.40
6		-3.93	-0.88	-2.52	2.41
7	-4.81		-1.54	-2.02	3.17
8	-3.78		-1.55	-2.02	2.66
9	-3.34		-1.85	-2.15	2.60
10	-1.84	-6.69		-1.68	4.27
11	-1.64	-5.66		-1.35	3.65
12	-1.51	-5.08		-1.07	3.29
Average	-3.62	-4.78	-2.67	-2.26	

We see that while the end of period market price in continuous double auctions deviated from the real value of the respective glass by on average 3.37 EUR in the first period, the market price in call auction markets deviated by on average 5.77 EUR from the real value in period 1. For a short time horizon in periods 5 and 6 the market price in the call auction market deviates on average less than the average deviation in the continuous double auction market. Afterwards the continuous double auction is way more efficient and closes with an average deviation in period 12 of 1.53 EUR compared to the call auction with an average deviation of 3.29 EUR in period 12. If we would exclude the observations for glass B, we see almost similar deviations on average at the end of the 12 trading periods in both market mechanisms.

If we now compare the pure average of the estimations like suggested by Hora et al. (2013), who aggregated simply the median of individual estimations as an aggregation mechanism of different information. Figures 15 and 16 show the results. We see that the deviation of the first informed estimation is on average at -4.2 EUR. Compared to both market mechanisms, the average deviation of estimations from real value is better than the average deviation of market prices in call auctions, but worse than continuous double auctions. This trend continues untill period 12, where the average of individual estimations is -2.69 EUR, in the continuous double auction 1.53 EUR, and in the call auction 3.29 EUR.

From table 14 it appears that simple averaging of individual estimations is compared to average market prices from treatment CDA worse in predicting the real value of assets. In period a, before any trading took place, participants from treatment CDA on average deviated with their estimations by -9.52 euros from the real value of the coins in the glasses. Participants from treatment CALL deviated with their estimations on average by -12.40 from the real value. This is interesting, as there has not been any trading yet, still there is a difference between those two groups. This allows for the thought that by chance participants in treatment CDA were better in estimating than participants in treatment CALL. The difference between estimations in both treatments declined steadily over all twelve trading periods. In periods d and 10 estimations from treatment group CALL were even slightly better than estimations from treatment group

CDA. Still, by comparing figure 15 that shows deviations of estimations and average market prices from real value in treatment group CDA to figure 16 that shows the same graphics for treatment CALL, we see that compared to the respective market prices estimations do not deviate as much from market prices in the CALL auction treatment as they do in treatment CDA. This indicates that participants in treatment CALL believed more in the accuracy of prices in call auction mechanisms than the CDA treatment group believed that the market price in continuous double auction markets reflects the true value of the coins in the glasses. We see that for both market mechanisms the average of estimations and market prices get closer together over the course of the twelve periods. This effect is more obvious for CALL auction mechanisms. Nevertheless, it can also be seen that the average market price of continuous double auctions achieves much more accuracy over all trading periods. But also the market price in treatment call gets closer to the real value through trading.

Table 15: Average Deviation of Market Prices and Estimations.

Period	Price CDA	Price CALL	Est. CDA	Est. CALL
a			-9.52	-12.40
1	0.02	-5.77	-5.22	-6.33
2	-1.76	-4.66	-4.51	-6.31
3	-2.22	-4.82	-4.21	-5.29
b			-6.32	-7.56
4	-2.10	-3.11	-3.60	-3.96
5	-2.61	-2.66	-3.08	-3.49
6	-2.53	-2.44	-3.19	-3.43
c			-4.87	-4.91
7	-0.75	-2.79	-3.08	-3.18
8	-1.81	-2.45	-2.57	-2.91
9	-1.38	-2.45	-2.14	-2.64
d			-5.59	-5.55
10	-1.78	-3.41	-3.12	-3.06
11	-1.89	-2.88	-2.60	-2.77
12	-1.53	-2.55	-2.60	-2.46

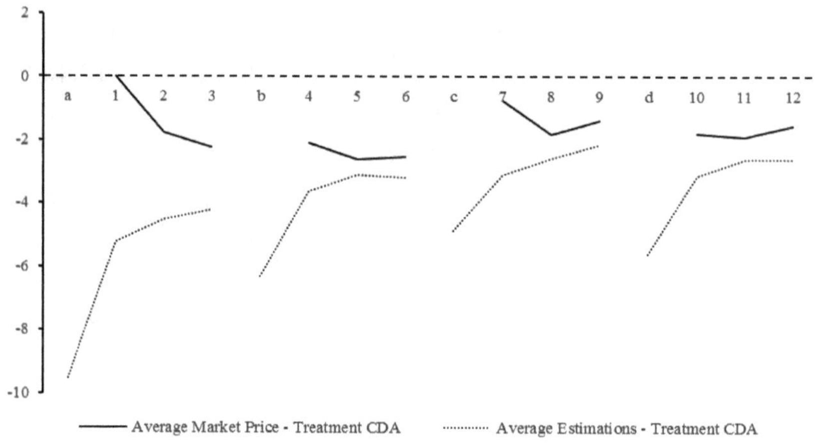

Figure 15: Comparison of Participants' Estimations of Glass Value and Resulting Market Prices in Trading Periods - Treatment CDA.

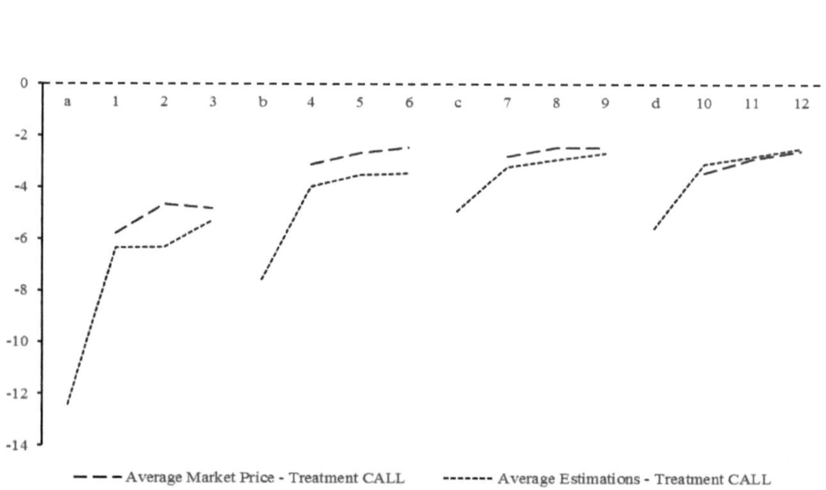

Figure 16: Comparison of Participants' Estimations of Glass Value and Resulting Market Prices in Trading Periods - Treatment CALL.

Conducting a regression analysis allows to get better insight what influences the magnitude of net profit achieved by participants in each period and thus the influencing factors for success. Formula 1 shows the parameters of the regression analysis.

$$Net\ Profit = \propto + \beta_{IL} * IL_i + \beta_{DoE} * DoE_i + \beta_{CDA} * CDA_i$$

The influence of deviation of estimations (DoE), the influence of participants' information level (IL), and the influence of the treatment (CDA) on net profit is tested. Deviation of estimations is measured as the deviation of estimations from the real value of the coins.

$$DoE = \ Estimation_{ij} - True\ Value_{ij}$$

In this equation i stands for the respective subject and j stands for the respective glass that is estimated and traded. Net profit is calculated as follows:

$$\begin{aligned} Net\ Profit = \ & Asset\ Value_{End} + Cash_{End} - Cash_{Begin} \\ & - Assets_{Begin} * Asset\ Value \end{aligned}$$

The influence of deviation of estimations on net profit is negative. Intuitively this means that the better an estimation, the smaller is the deviation from the real value, and the better will the net profit be. Still the magnitude of this influence is not big. The influence of information level on net profit is much bigger and positive. This is reasonable as better informed traders get a higher net profit. A participant gets 3.03 euros more net profit for each additional information level. In continuous double auctions a subject gets on average

5.93 euros more than a subject in call auction treatment. A participant with information level 0 and no deviation of estimations from real value earns 18.68 euros net profit in treatment CDA. In treatment CALL the same participant would earn only 12.75 euros. Table 15 shows the the regression statistics. Table 16 shows the overall results of this regression analysis.

Table 16: Regression Statistics - Influencing Factors for Net Profit.

Multiple R	0.15
R Square	0.02
Adjusted R Square	0.02
Standard Error	45.06
Observations	1728

Table 17: Regression Analysis - Influencing Factors for Net Profit.

	Coefficients	Standard Error	T Stat	p-value
Intercept	15.10	2.84	5.31	0.00
Deviation of Estimation	-1.17	0.22	-5.30	0.00
Information Level	3.07	1.04	2.94	0.00
CDA	5.49	2.18	2.51	0.01
Gender	-4.10	2.20	-1.86	0.06

Now it would be interesting if this development of additional net profit with additional information level is linear, or if big jumps are observable between information levels. From table 17 we see that net profit highly depends on information level. While we saw a general positive trend for information level leading to higher net profit in the previous regression analyses, this trend is not linear. Overall, we see that net profit increases from I0 to I1 by 0.12, from I1 to I2 by 9.44, but from I2 to I3 it decreases by 9.31 on average. This indicates that more information is not always better, but is not in line with the J-curve effect (Schredelseker, 1984). This effect would imply that I0 has the best net profit and all other participants earn less except a complete insider. As we do not have any complete insiders in our experiment this effect cannot be observed. Additionally, participants might be influenced by previous information that they received in previous rounds. In treatment CDA net profit increases from I0 to I1 by 3.89, from I1 to I2 by 15.29, but from I2 to I3 it decreases by 16.72 on average. In treatment CALL net profits decrease from I0 to I1 by 3.64, increase from I1 to I2 by 3.60, and decrease again I2 to I3 by 1.90 on average. Information seems to play a much more important role in continuous double auctions than in call auctions and is much more worth there. This can also be seen in figure 17. We still must keep in mind, that participants that have I0 in one period might have had I3 in previous periods and as all glasses have a value between 20 and 30 Euros participants might be influenced by previously received information.

Table 18: Net Profit depending on Information Level.

	I0	I1	I2	I3
Net Profit CDA	20.67	24.56	39.05	23.13
Net Profit CALL	23.10	19.45	23.05	21.15
Overall	21.88	22.01	31.45	22.14
Deviation	-2.43	5.11	16.80	1.97
Additional CDA		3.89	15.29	-16.72
Additional CALL		-3.64	3.60	-1.90
Additional Overall		0.12	9.44	-9.31

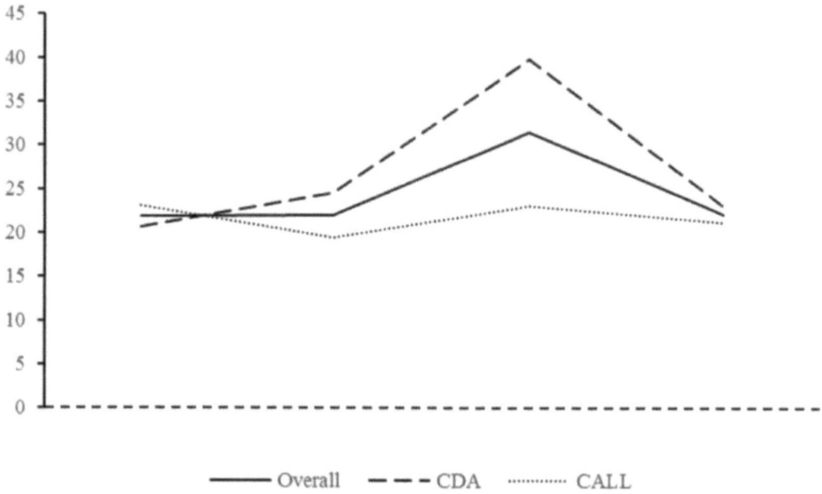

Figure 17: Net Profit depending on Information Level.

4.4 Trading Volume and Net Change of Assets

Another important factor when comparing both market mechanisms are differences in trading volume. Figure 18 shows the net change of assets in treatment CALL and treatment CDA. Net change of assets is calculated as all transacted bids.

It is apparent that for treatment CDA the net change of assets is much higher than for treatment CALL. This can also be seen in tables 18 and 19.

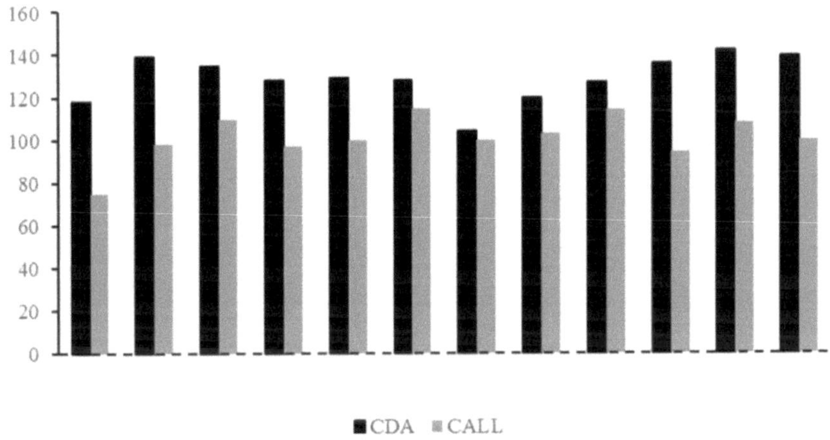

Figure 18: Net Change of Assets.

Table 19: Net Change of Assets - Treatment CDA.

Period/ Markets	1	2	3	4	5	6	7	8	9	Overall
1	10	13	11	20	11	16	12	13	12	118
2	14	16	11	23	10	20	15	16	14	139
3	15	19	9	22	11	16	16	16	11	135
4	13	15	9	20	9	14	16	19	13	128
5	10	19	11	13	10	20	13	18	15	129
6	13	18	11	11	6	21	17	16	15	128
7	10	14	16	9	5	12	6	16	16	104
8	11	15	12	16	9	15	9	18	15	120
9	16	15	19	12	10	15	5	18	17	127
10	6	20	17	20	12	14	12	19	16	136
11	14	17	18	19	15	15	9	15	20	142
12	10	19	17	17	18	17	7	13	21	139
Overall	142	200	161	202	126	195	137	197	185	1545

Table 20: Net Change of Assets - Treatment CALL.

Period/ Markets	1	2	3	4	5	6	7	8	9	Overall
1	7	8	12	6	6	11	9	11	5	75
2	3	16	17	6	11	16	7	12	10	98
3	3	20	14	9	15	14	6	10	19	110
4	11	9	14	11	10	14	5	8	15	97
5	9	10	10	9	8	20	7	7	20	100
6	9	17	16	6	8	18	12	10	19	115
7	6	14	12	9	17	13	8	9	12	100
8	10	13	7	12	15	20	4	4	18	103
9	5	12	12	11	16	20	11	2	25	114
10	5	12	5	19	16	10	10	3	14	94
11	3	15	5	14	15	11	13	7	25	108
12	4	20	9	11	13	13	10	5	15	100
Overall	75	166	133	123	150	180	102	88	197	1214

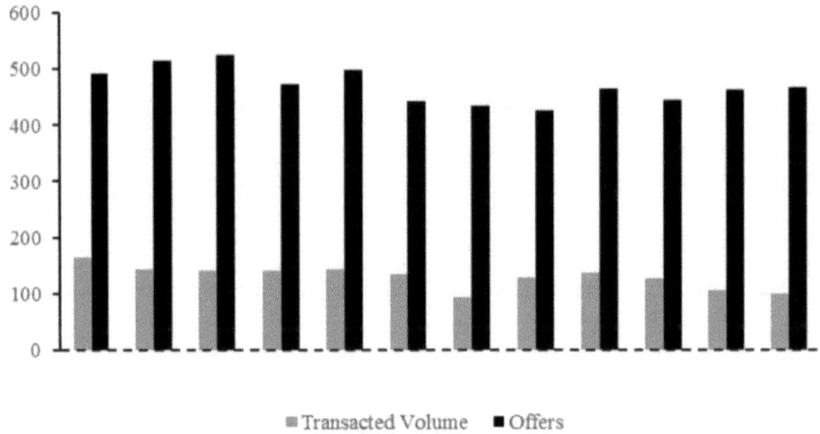

Figure 19: Trading Volume - Treatment CDA.

For treatment CALL net change of assets also is the trading volume, as assets are only traded once at the end of the period and thus there is no change of assets during trading periods. In treatment CDA assets are changed ongoing. Table 20 shows all offers and all offers that actually led to a transaction. Two things can be seen. First, the number of offers that were never transacted is much higher than the number of transactions that were transacted. Second, the trading volume in treatment CDA is much higher than just the net change of asstes at the end of each trading period.

Table 21: Net Profit depending on Information Level.

Period	Offers	Transactions
1	492	163
2	516	143
3	526	141
4	474	140
5	498	142
6	443	135
7	435	93
8	426	129
9	466	136
10	444	126
11	463	106
12	468	99
Overall	5651	1553

4.5 Critique and Ideas for Future Research

Critically observed, one must state that students as participants are possibly not the most representative subjects. Still, Larrick et al. (2011) state that the most important factor to observe a wisdom of the crowd phenomenon is that subjects are properly incentivized. Through paying students in this experiment that is fulfilled. Further Herzog and Hertwig (2009) demand mixing of participants with different backgrounds for observing wisdom of the crowd. Students come from all countries to study in this university, so they have diverse backgrounds. Still, there is a tendency that most students are

WEIRD - western, educated, industrialized, rich, and democratic societies which leads to a subject pool that is about the same age, is of over average intelligence, and might not be representative. Of course, this experiment took place in a lab and thus might not be completely applicable in the real world. Still, Lorenz et al. (2011) argue that even mild social influence destroys wisdom of the crowd. In a lab surrounding it is possible to rule out this kind of influence. Thus, this experiment is a pretty good and representative analysis of the phenomenon of wisdom of the crowd.

According to Hakanes (2014), crowd funding can be used as a tool to aggregate vague information. An idea for future research could be to test the ability of crowd funding as a tool to aggregate information in comparison to the market mechanisms tested in the experiment of this thesis.
Another idea could be to analyze possible behavioral influences on the efficiency of the information aggregation mechanisms. Galinsky and Mussweiler (2001) provide a study where they give first offers as possible anchors prior to the actual experiment. It could be interesting to analyze how well call auctions or double auctions still aggregate information in case that individuals are biased. Another idea could be to involve subjects' emotions and test the implications for different market mechanisms like Hirshleifer and Shumway (2003) did for the influence of emotions on asset prices.
It could also be interesting to add information costs in the experiment to test whether the crowd is less wise in case it has no information unless it must pay for it (Grossman et al. 1976). Barreda et al. (2016a) provide in their experiment additionally the possibility to share information prior to the experiment. Ferri and Morone (2014)

introduce rating agencies. This would all be interesting to test the efficiency of market mechanisms in these cases and whether wisdom of the crowd is still possible.

5 Conclusion

In this thesis, I set up a lab experiment to explore differences in market mechanisms regarding their ability to aggregate information effectively. The tested market mechanisms were call auctions and continuous double auctions. Subjects were asked to estimate the value of glasses filled with coins while receiving different information about the coins in the glasses. Afterwards those glasses were traded in either a call auction market or a continuous double auction mechanism. The main goal was to analyze in which market mechanism the phenomenon of wisdom of the crowd is better observable.

Overall a clear tendency of under estimation of the glass value is apparent and the intuition that it seems rather difficult to estimate the value of a glass filled with coins without any further information. Most likely this also holds for the valuation of stocks. Without any information about the company, only by looking at it, it seems almost impossible to estimate the stock value. This fact supports the appropriateness of the conducted experiment and its settings as a representative market situation.

We see that trading distributes information effectively in both treatments - CALL and CDA. This can be seen from a decreasing standard deviation over all trading periods and deceasing average deviations of estimations from real value over time. Compared to treatment CALL distribution of information takes place faster in treatment CDA. Still, at the end this effect diminishes and both estimations, from participants of treatment CALL and treatment CDA,

L. K. Senninger, *Wisdom of the Crowd in Experiments*, BestMasters,
https://doi.org/10.1007/978-3-658-24294-7_5

have the same average deviation from real value. This is only a small effect and since this effect exists from the beginning, before trading took place, this might be a general effect that one group just estimated better.

During trading market prices from treatment CDA as well as market prices from treatment CALL converged to the true value of the asset. Nevertheless, this convergence is much faster and better in treatment CDA. Only in this treatment the deviation of market prices reaches zero in most markets at the end of trading. In treatment CALL two out of nine market prices reach a deviation from real asset value of about zero, the prices in all other markets still deviate from the asset value at the end of trading.

Additionally, in continuous double auctions prices react faster and much more flexible to changes. In this experiment glass B with an extraordinary higher value than the other glasses is traded at a reasonable price much faster than in treatment CALL. Call auctions also show some reactions and the same tendency, but it takes much more time to implement such a change.

Through regression analyses we showed that the net profit is influenced by the deviation of estimations and the information level of participants. The influence of information is thereby much higher than the goodness of estimations. Additionally, both effects are more pronounced in treatment CDA than in treatment CALL. This indicates that information is more valuable in continuous double auctions than in call auctions. Information can be used better to get higher profits in treatment CDA. Also, the net profit is on average higher in treatment CALL than in treatment CDA, if one has no information.

We also see that estimations and prices converge over time. This implies that information is distributed through trading and that traders act according to their estimations of the real value of the asset. Still, market prices in treatment CDA are strictly better than the average of estimations. Market prices in treatment CALL are at the beginning better in predicting the asset value than the average of estimations, but worse at the end. This implies that continuous double auctions are best able to use for the wisdom of the crowd effect, as the individual believes are aggregated in the fastest way and the most effective way. In the short run, call auctions are second best in aggregating information after continuous double auctions as the market price in the short run was better than the average of individual guesses. In the long run, the average of individual guesses reacts faster and thus is better able to predict the true value.

6 Appendix

Innsbruck
EconLab

Liebe ExperimentteilnehmerInnen,

herzlich willkommen beim heutigen Experiment.

Bitte lesen Sie die Anleitungen zum Experiment genau durch. Alle Aussagen in den Anleitungen entsprechen der Wahrheit. Die Höhe Ihrer Auszahlung am Ende des Experiments hängt auch davon ab, wie gut Sie die Anleitungen verstanden haben. Wenn Sie eine Frage haben, zeigen Sie bitte auf. Ihre Frage wird dann privat beantwortet. Das Experiment sowie die Auswertung der Daten erfolgen anonym.

Wir bitten Sie, von nun an nicht mehr mit anderen TeilnehmerInnen zu sprechen und nur jene Hilfsmittel zu verwenden, die von den ExperimentleiterInnen zur Verfügung gestellt wurden. Bitte schalten Sie daher alle elektronischen Geräte aus. Am Computer dürfen ebenso nur Funktionen verwendet werden, die für das Experiment notwendig sind. Bei Verstößen gegen diese Regeln erhalten Sie keine Auszahlung und werden von zukünftigen Experimenten ausgeschlossen.

Vielen Dank für Ihre Aufmerksamkeit und Ihre Teilnahme am heutigen Experiment.

Ablauf des Experiments:

Dieses Experiment besteht aus zwei Teilen – einem Marktexperiment und einem Abschlussexperiment, das weitere kurze Entscheidungssituationen umfasst. In beiden Experimentteilen können Sie Geld verdienen. Vor Beginn der Experimente werden Sie in getrennten Einleitungen mit den Regeln vertraut gemacht.

Experiment 1: Marktexperiment

- Einleitung zum Handelsbildschirm
- Probeperiode
- Einleitung zu den gehandelten Assets
- Experiment
- Fragebogen

Experiment 2: Abschlussexperiment

- Einleitung und Experiment
- Fragebogen

Auszahlung

L. K. Senninger, *Wisdom of the Crowd in Experiments*, BestMasters,
https://doi.org/10.1007/978-3-658-24294-7

(1) EINLEITUNG ZUM HANDELSBILDSCHIRM:

Sie können in diesem Experiment mit Münzen (1€, 20, 5 und 1 Cent) gefüllte Gläser kaufen und verkaufen. Genauere Informationen zu diesen Gläsern erhalten Sie nach zwei Probeperioden. Gehandelt wird in Form einer beidseitigen Auktion. Dies bedeutet, dass jeder Händler sowohl als Käufer als auch als Verkäufer auftreten kann. Dazu können Sie in jeder Periode beliebig viele Kauf- sowie Verkaufsgebote abgeben, indem Sie einen Preis eingeben, zu dem Sie zu handeln bereit sind (mit maximal zwei Kommastellen; das Kommazeichen ist der Punkt). Jedes Gebot ist dabei für genau 1 Glas gefüllt mit Münzen.

Wenn Sie mit der Erstellung Ihrer Kauf- und Verkaufsgebote fertig sind, können Sie diese mit dem Button „Gebote abschicken" an den Markt senden. Dieser ermittelt aus den Geboten aller Händler einen einheitlichen Preis, so dass die Anzahl der ge- bzw. verkauften Gläser gleich ist. Setzen Sie einige hohe Kaufgebote, so steigt dadurch tendenziell der Preis und vice versa. Alle Kaufgebote mit Preisen über diesem einheitlichen Preis sowie alle Verkaufsgebote mit Preisen unter diesem einheitlichen Preis werden zum einheitlichen Preis abgewickelt, d.h. Sie verkaufen so viele Gläser wie sie unter diesem Preis angeboten haben und kaufen so viele Gläser wie Sie Gebote über diesem Preis gesetzt haben. Pro Glas das Sie ***kaufen*** wird Ihr Eurobestand um den Preis verringert und Ihr Bestand an Gläsern um 1 erhöht und vice versa für jedes Glas das Sie ***verkaufen***.

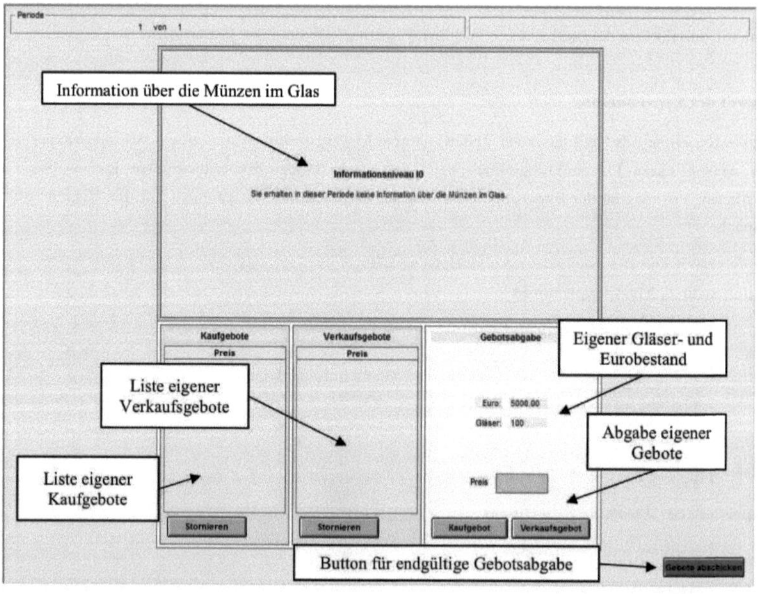

Um Sie mit der Funktionsweise des Handelssystems vertraut zu machen, führen wir nun zwei Probeperioden zu jeweils 2 Minuten durch. Nutzen Sie diese, um den Umgang mit dem Handelssystem zu trainieren. Die Probeperioden sind nicht auszahlungsrelevant. Nach jeder Probeperiode sehen Sie, wie viele Gläser Sie zu verschiedenen möglichen Preisen ge- bzw. verkauft hätten.

(2) ABLAUF DES EXPERIMENTS:

Das Experiment ist in insgesamt **12 Perioden** zu je 3 Minuten gegliedert. Zur Erinnerung: Sie können in diesem Experiment mit Münzen (1€, 20, 5 und 1 Cent) gefüllte Gläser kaufen und verkaufen. Jeder Teilnehmer startet jede Periode mit einer Ausstattung von 5 Gläsern und einem gewissen Eurobestand. Nicht jeder Händler erhält jede Periode gleich viele Euro. Der Handelskurs des Glases bestimmt sich aus Angebot und Nachfrage von Ihnen und den anderen sieben Händlern in Ihrer Reihe (es handeln immer nur die acht Händler in einer Reihe miteinander).

Sie handeln jedes Glas (gesamt gibt es 4 verschiedene, genannt A, B, C, D) für drei aufeinanderfolgende Perioden, wobei Ihre Anfangsausstattung jede Periode 5 Gläser und einen Eurobetrag beträgt.

	Perioden 1-3	Perioden 4-6	Perioden 7-9	Perioden 10-12
Reihe 1	Glastyp A	Glastyp B	Glastyp C	Glastyp D
Reihe 2	Glastyp B	Glastyp C	Glastyp D	Glastyp A
Reihe 3	Glastyp C	Glastyp D	Glastyp A	Glastyp B
nicht benutzt	Glastyp D	Glastyp A	Glastyp B	Glastyp C

Zu Beginn eines 3-Perioden-Blocks werden Gläser des entsprechenden Typs zur Begutachtung durch die Teilnehmer ausgeteilt (jeweils acht Teilnehmer erhalten das gleiche Glas, wobei jeder es für 15 Sekunden betrachten, drehen, etc. kann). Nach 3 Handelsperioden wird denselben acht Personen ein anderes Glas zur Begutachtung ausgehändigt. Nachdem Sie das Glas betrachtet haben werden Sie gebeten am Computer eine Schätzung des Gesamtwerts aller Münzen im Glas abzugeben.

Nachdem Sie diese erste Schätzung abgegeben haben, erfahren Sie am Bildschirm die Anzahl und den Wert verschiedener Münzarten, die in dem Glas enthalten sind. Insgesamt gibt es vier Informationsniveaus (I0, I1, I2 und I3). Je zwei der acht Teilnehmer einer Reihe erhalten drei Perioden lang dieselbe Information (im Markt sind also je 2 Mal I0, I1, I2 und I3). Je nach Informationsniveau erfahren Sie die Anzahl keiner, einer oder mehrerer Münzarten, die in dem Glas enthalten sind. Außerdem erfahren Sie den Wert dieser Münzen. Ein Teilnehmer mit Informationsniveau I0 erfährt nichts über die Anzahl an Münzen; I1 erfährt Anzahl und Wert der 1€-Münzen; I2 Anzahl und Wert der 1€- sowie der 20 Cent-Münzen, und I3 (der Bestinformierte) Anzahl und Wert der 1€-, 20 Cent- und 5 Cent-Münzen. Niemand erfährt Anzahl oder Wert der 1 Cent-Münzen. Die Informationsstruktur sieht also wie folgt aus:

	1€	20 Cent	5 Cent	1 Cent
I0				
I1	bekannt			
I2	bekannt	bekannt		

I3	bekannt	bekannt	bekannt	

Nachdem Sie die Information erhalten haben, werden Sie erneut gebeten, eine Schätzung des Werts aller Münzen im Glas abzugeben. Auch zu Beginn von Perioden, in denen kein neues Glas ausgeteilt wird, müssen Sie nochmals den Wert der Münzen im zuletzt ausgeteilten Glas schätzen. Für jede Schätzung erhalten Sie am Ende des Experiments 20 Cent ausbezahlt, wenn die Schätzung um maximal 5% vom tatsächlichen Wert der Münzen im Glas abweicht, 10 Cent, wenn die Schätzung um maximal 15% abweicht, und 5 Cent, wenn die Schätzung um maximal 25% abweicht. Insgesamt können Sie durch die Schätzungen weitere 3 Euro verdienen. Nach der Abgabe Ihrer Schätzung startet der Handel.

Nach 3 Handelsperioden bekommen die Teilnehmer Informationen über den neuen Glastyp, wobei sich auch das jeweilige Informationsniveau ändert. Jeder Teilnehmer wird einmal jedes Informationsniveau erhalten, das bedeutet niemand ist über die Gesamtdauer des Experiments besser oder schlechter gestellt. Der Handel ist in jeder Periode gleich aufgebaut. Sie können jeweils entscheiden, ob Sie Gläser an andere Teilnehmer verkaufen oder von anderen Teilnehmern kaufen wollen.

(3) ÜBERSICHTSBILDSCHIRM:

Nach Ablauf der Handelszeit sehen Sie einen Übersichtsbildschirm, der Ihnen die Anzahl an Gläsern sowie Ihren Eurobestand am Periodenende zeigt. Sie beginnen jede Periode wieder mit 5 Gläsern und einem gewissen Eurobetrag. Nach je 3 aufeinanderfolgenden Perioden beginnen Sie mit einem neuen Glas (A, B, C oder D) und einem neuen Informationsniveau (I0, I1, I2 oder I3).

(4) AUSZAHLUNG:

Nachdem alle 12 Perioden beendet sind, wird Ihre Auszahlung auf Grundlage der von Ihnen in einer (zufällig gewählten) der 12 Perioden erhandelten Gläser und Ihrem Eurovermögen berechnet. Dabei wird Ihr Endvermögen (= Eurobestand plus Wert der Münzen in den jeweiligen Gläsern) in einer zufällig ausgewählten Periode bestimmt und durch 30 dividiert. Dies ergibt den Eurobetrag, den Sie aus dem Handelsteil des Marktexperiments verdient haben. Dazu kommt der Eurobetrag, den sie aus Ihren Schätzungen der Werte der Münzen in den Gläsern verdient haben. Die Summe dieser beiden Beträge bekommen Sie ausbezahlt.

Noch mal die wichtigsten Details zum Experiment:

- Es gibt 12 Handelsperioden, wobei sie je drei aufeinanderfolgenden Perioden dasselbe Glas handeln (insgesamt vier verschiedene Gläser A, B, C und D).
- Jeder Teilnehmer startet jede Periode mit 5 Gläsern und einem bestimmten Eurobestand.
- Es gibt vier Informationsniveaus I0, I1, I2 und I3. Jeweils zwei Teilnehmer in einer Sitzreihe erhalten das gleiche Informationsniveau über den Inhalt der Gläser. Im Laufe der 12 Perioden hat jeder Teilnehmer jedes Informationsniveau einmal für drei Perioden.
- Jedes Glas zahlt nach der Periode den exakten Wert der enthaltenen Münzen.
- Die finale Auszahlung errechnet sich aus dem wahren Wert der Gläser und Ihrem Eurobestand in einer der 12 Perioden (zufällig gewählt), dividiert durch 30. Dazu kommt noch die Entlohnung für die Schätzungen (bis zu 3 Euro).

Innsbruck EconLab

Liebe ExperimentteilnehmerInnen,

herzlich willkommen beim heutigen Experiment.

Bitte lesen Sie die Anleitungen zum Experiment genau durch. Alle Aussagen in den Anleitungen entsprechen der Wahrheit. Die Höhe Ihrer Auszahlung am Ende des Experiments hängt auch davon ab, wie gut Sie die Anleitungen verstanden haben. Wenn Sie eine Frage haben, zeigen Sie bitte auf. Ihre Frage wird dann privat beantwortet. Das Experiment sowie die Auswertung der Daten erfolgen anonym.

Wir bitten Sie, von nun an nicht mehr mit anderen TeilnehmerInnen zu sprechen und nur jene Hilfsmittel zu verwenden, die von den ExperimentleiterInnen zur Verfügung gestellt wurden. Bitte schalten Sie daher alle elektronischen Geräte aus. Am Computer dürfen ebenso nur Funktionen verwendet werden, die für das Experiment notwendig sind. Bei Verstößen gegen diese Regeln erhalten Sie keine Auszahlung und werden von zukünftigen Experimenten ausgeschlossen.

Vielen Dank für Ihre Aufmerksamkeit und Ihre Teilnahme am heutigen Experiment.

Ablauf des Experiments:

Dieses Experiment besteht aus zwei Teilen – einem Marktexperiment und einem Abschlussexperiment, das weitere kurze Entscheidungssituationen umfasst. In beiden Experimentteilen können Sie Geld verdienen. Vor Beginn der Experimente werden Sie in getrennten Einleitungen mit den Regeln vertraut gemacht.

Experiment 1: Marktexperiment

Einleitung zum Handelsbildschirm

Probeperiode

Einleitung zu den gehandelten Assets

Experiment

Fragebogen

Experiment 2: Abschlussexperiment

Einleitung und Experiment

Fragebogen

Auszahlung

(1) EINLEITUNG ZUM HANDELSBILDSCHIRM:

Sie können in diesem Experiment mit Münzen (1€, 20, 5 und 1 Cent) gefüllte Gläser kaufen und verkaufen. Genauere Informationen zu diesen Gläsern erhalten Sie nach der Probeperiode. Gehandelt wird in Form einer kontinuierlichen, beidseitigen Auktion. Dies bedeutet, dass jeder Händler sowohl als Käufer als auch als Verkäufer auftreten kann. Dazu können Sie beliebig viele Kauf- sowie Verkaufsgebote abgeben, indem Sie einen Preis eingeben, zu dem Sie zu handeln bereit sind (mit maximal zwei Kommastellen; das Kommazeichen ist der Punkt) und dann „Kaufgebot/Verkaufsgebot" klicken um ein Kaufgebot/Verkaufsgebot abzugeben. Jedes Gebot ist dabei für genau 1 Glas gefüllt mit Münzen.

Alle Gebote werden der Höhe nach sortiert, so dass stets das Beste oben steht und blau hinterlegt ist. Das jeweils beste Gebot kann mit dem Button „Kauf" bzw. „Verkauf" akzeptiert werden. Wenn Sie ein Glas ***kaufen***, so wird Ihr Eurobestand um den jeweiligen Preis verringert und Ihr Bestand an Gläsern um 1 erhöht. Umgekehrt, wenn Sie ein Glas ***verkaufen***, so wird Ihr Eurobestand um den Verkaufspreis erhöht und Ihr Bestand an Gläsern um 1 verringert.

Bitte beachten Sie, dass Sie nur so viele Gläser kaufen (verkaufen) können, wie mit Ihrem Eurobestand (Gläser-Bestand) gedeckt sind. Negative Bestände von Euro oder Gläsern (Leerverkäufe) sind also nicht zulässig. Der Computer löscht Gebote, die nicht mehr gedeckt sind.

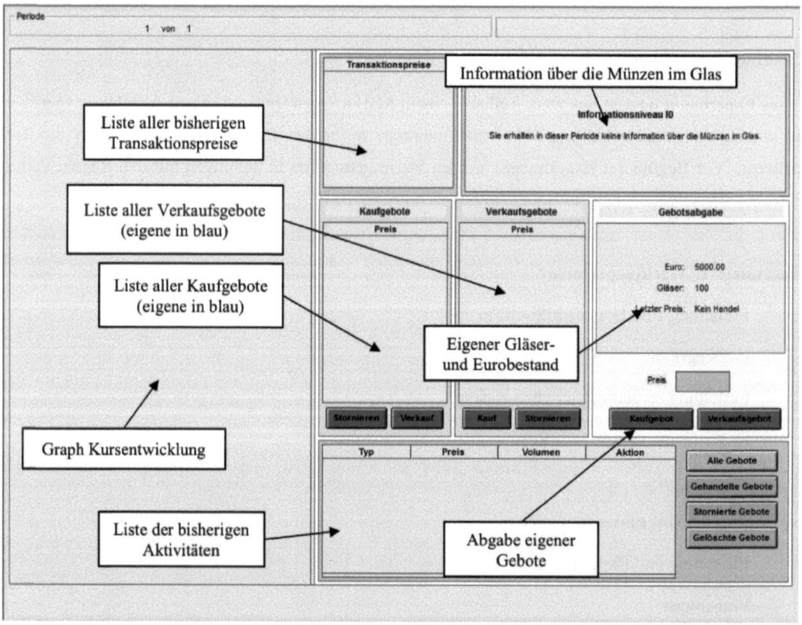

Um Sie mit der Funktionsweise des Handelssystems vertraut zu machen, führen wir nun eine Probeperiode von 5 Minuten durch. Nutzen Sie diese, um den Umgang mit dem Handelssystem zu trainieren. Die Probeperiode ist nicht auszahlungsrelevant.

(2) ABLAUF DES EXPERIMENTS:

Das Experiment ist in insgesamt **12 Perioden** zu je 3 Minuten gegliedert. Zur Erinnerung: Sie können in diesem Experiment mit Münzen (1€, 20, 5 und 1 Cent) gefüllte Gläser kaufen und verkaufen. Jeder Teilnehmer startet jede Periode mit einer Ausstattung von 5 Gläsern und einem gewissen Eurobestand. Nicht jeder Händler erhält jede Periode gleich viele Euro. Der Handelskurs des Glases bestimmt sich aus Angebot und Nachfrage von Ihnen und den anderen sieben Händlern in Ihrer Reihe (es handeln immer nur die acht Händler in einer Reihe miteinander).

Sie handeln jedes Glas (gesamt gibt es 4 verschiedene, genannt A, B, C, D) für drei aufeinanderfolgende Perioden, wobei Ihre Anfangsausstattung jede Periode 5 Gläser und einen Eurobetrag beträgt.

	Perioden 1-3	Perioden 4-6	Perioden 7-9	Perioden 10-12
Reihe 1	Glastyp A	Glastyp B	Glastyp C	Glastyp D
Reihe 2	Glastyp B	Glastyp C	Glastyp D	Glastyp A
Reihe 3	Glastyp C	Glastyp D	Glastyp A	Glastyp B
nicht benutzt	Glastyp D	Glastyp A	Glastyp B	Glastyp C

Zu Beginn eines 3-Perioden-Blocks werden Gläser des entsprechenden Typs zur Begutachtung durch die Teilnehmer ausgeteilt (jeweils acht Teilnehmer erhalten das gleiche Glas, wobei jeder es für 15 Sekunden betrachten, drehen, etc. kann). Nach 3 Handelsperioden wird denselben acht Personen ein anderes Glas zur Begutachtung ausgehändigt. Nachdem Sie das Glas betrachtet haben werden Sie gebeten am Computer eine Schätzung des Gesamtwerts aller Münzen im Glas abzugeben.

Nachdem Sie diese erste Schätzung abgegeben haben, erfahren Sie am Bildschirm die Anzahl und den Wert verschiedener Münzarten, die in dem Glas enthalten sind. Insgesamt gibt es vier Informationsniveaus (I0, I1, I2 und I3). Je zwei der acht Teilnehmer einer Reihe erhalten drei Perioden lang dieselbe Information (im Markt sind also je 2 Mal I0, I1, I2 und I3). Je nach Informationsniveau erfahren Sie die Anzahl keiner, einer oder mehrerer Münzarten, die in dem Glas enthalten sind. Außerdem erfahren Sie den Wert dieser Münzen. Ein Teilnehmer mit Informationsniveau I0 erfährt nichts über die Anzahl an Münzen; I1 erfährt Anzahl und Wert der 1€-Münzen; I2 Anzahl und Wert der 1€- sowie der 20 Cent-Münzen, und I3 (der Bestinformierte) Anzahl und Wert der 1€-, 20 Cent- und 5 Cent-Münzen. Niemand erfährt Anzahl oder Wert der 1 Cent-Münzen. Die Informationsstruktur sieht also wie folgt aus:

	1€	20 Cent	5 Cent	1 Cent
I0				
I1	bekannt			
I2	bekannt	bekannt		

I3	bekannt	bekannt	bekannt	

Nachdem Sie die Information erhalten haben, werden Sie erneut gebeten, eine Schätzung des Werts aller Münzen im Glas abzugeben. Auch zu Beginn von Perioden, in denen kein neues Glas ausgeteilt wird, müssen Sie nochmals den Wert der Münzen im zuletzt ausgeteilten Glas schätzen. Für jede Schätzung erhalten Sie am Ende des Experiments 20 Cent ausbezahlt, wenn die Schätzung um maximal 5% vom tatsächlichen Wert der Münzen im Glas abweicht, 10 Cent, wenn die Schätzung um maximal 15% abweicht, und 5 Cent, wenn die Schätzung um maximal 25% abweicht. Insgesamt können Sie durch die Schätzungen weitere 3 Euro verdienen. Nach der Abgabe Ihrer Schätzung startet der Handel.
Nach 3 Handelsperioden bekommen die Teilnehmer Informationen über den neuen Glastyp, wobei sich auch das jeweilige Informationsniveau ändert. Jeder Teilnehmer wird einmal jedes Informationsniveau erhalten, das bedeutet niemand ist über die Gesamtdauer des Experiments besser oder schlechter gestellt.
Der Handel ist in jeder Periode gleich aufgebaut. Sie können jeweils entscheiden, ob Sie Gläser an andere Teilnehmer verkaufen oder von anderen Teilnehmern kaufen wollen.

(3) ÜBERSICHTSBILDSCHIRM:

Nach Ablauf der Handelszeit sehen Sie einen Übersichtsbildschirm, der Ihnen die Anzahl an Gläsern sowie Ihren Eurobestand am Periodenende zeigt. Sie beginnen jede Periode wieder mit 5 Gläsern und einem gewissen Eurobetrag. Nach je 3 aufeinanderfolgenden Perioden beginnen Sie mit einem neuen Glas (A, B, C oder D) und einem neuen Informationsniveau (I0, I1, I2 oder I3).

(4) AUSZAHLUNG:

Nachdem alle 12 Perioden beendet sind, wird Ihre Auszahlung auf Grundlage der von Ihnen in einer (zufällig gewählten) der 12 Perioden erhandelten Gläser und Ihrem Eurovermögen berechnet. Dabei wird Ihr Endvermögen (= Eurobestand plus Wert der Münzen in den jeweiligen Gläsern) in einer zufällig ausgewählten Periode bestimmt und durch 30 dividiert. Dies ergibt den Eurobetrag, den Sie aus dem Handelsteil des Marktexperiments verdient haben. Dazu kommt der Eurobetrag, den sie aus Ihren Schätzungen der Werte der Münzen in den Gläsern verdient haben. Die Summe dieser beiden Beträge bekommen Sie ausbezahlt.

Noch mal die wichtigsten Details zum Experiment:

- Es gibt 12 Handelsperioden, wobei sie je drei aufeinanderfolgenden Perioden dasselbe Glas handeln (insgesamt vier verschiedene Gläser A, B, C und D).
- Jeder Teilnehmer startet jede Periode mit 5 Gläsern und einem bestimmten Eurobestand.
- Es gibt vier Informationsniveaus I0, I1, I2 und I3. Jeweils zwei Teilnehmer in einer Sitzreihe erhalten das gleiche Informationsniveau über den Inhalt der Gläser. Im Laufe der 12 Perioden hat jeder Teilnehmer jedes Informationsniveau einmal für drei Perioden.
- Jedes Glas zahlt nach der Periode den exakten Wert der enthaltenen Münzen.
- Die finale Auszahlung errechnet sich aus dem wahren Wert der Gläser und Ihrem Eurobestand in einer der 12 Perioden (zufällig gewählt), dividiert durch 30. Dazu kommt noch die Entlohnung für die Schätzungen (bis zu 3 Euro).

7 References

Amihud, Y., Mendelson, H., Lauterbach, B., 1997. Market microstructure and securities values: Evidence from the Tel Aviv Stock Exchange. Journal of Financial Economics 45 (3), 365-390.

Bacidore, J. M., Lipson, M. L., 2001. The effects of opening and closing procedures on the NYSE and Nasdaq. Afa 2001 New Orleans meeting, University of Georgia.

Barclay, M. J., Hendershott, T., Jones, C.M., 2008. Order consolidation, price efficiency, and extreme liquidity shocks. Journal of Financial and Quantitative Analysis 43 (01), 93-121.

Barreda-Tarrazona, I., Grimalda, G., Morone, A., Nuzzo, S., and Teglio, A., 2016a. Centralizing information increases market efficiency more than sharing information: results from experimental asset markets. Mimeo.

Bettman, J. R., M. F. Luce, J.W. Payne., 1998. Constructive consumer choice processes. J. Consumer Res. 25 (2) 187-217.

Budescu, D. V., 2006. Confidence in aggregation of opinions from multiple sources. K. Fiedler, P. Juslin, eds. Information sampling and adaptive cognition. Cambridge University Press, Cambridge, UK, 327-352.

L. K. Senninger, *Wisdom of the Crowd in Experiments*, BestMasters,
https://doi.org/10.1007/978-3-658-24294-7

Budescu, D. V., and Chen, E., 2014. Identifying expertise to extract the wisdom of crowds. Management Science, 61(2), 267-280.

Cain, D.M., Loewenstein, G., Moore, D.A., 2005. The dirt on coming clean: perverse effects of disclosing conflicts of interest. Journal of Legal Studies 34 (1), 1-25.

Cason, T.N., and Friedman, D., 1996. Price formation in double auction markets. Journal of Economic Dynamics and Control, 20 (8), 1307-1337.

Cason, T. N., Friedmann, D., 2008. A Comparison of Market Institutions. In: Plott, C. R., Smith, V. L. (Eds.), Handbook of Experimental Economics Results. Vol. 1. Elsevier, pp. 264-272.

Chang, R. P., Rhee, S. G., Stone, G. R., Tang, N., 2008. How does the call market method affect price efficiency? Evidence from the Singapore Stock Market. Journal of Banking & Finance 32 (10), 2205-2219.

Clemen, R.T., 1989. Combining forecasts: A review and annotated bibliography. International journal of forecasting, 5(4), pp.559-583.

Copeland, T.E. and Friedman, D., 1992. The market value of information: Some experimental results. Journal of Business, pp.241-266.

Davis-Stober, C.P., Budescu, D.V., Dana, J. and Broomell, S.B., 2014. When is a crowd wise? Decision, 1(2), p.79.

Davis, D. D., and Williams, A. W., 1986. The effects of rent asymmetries in posted offer markets. Journal of Economic Behavior and Organization, 7(3), 303-316.

Diamond, D.W. and Verrecchia, R.E., 1981. Information aggregation in a noisy rational expectations economy. Journal of Financial Economics, 9(3), 221-235.

Easley, D., Ledyard, J., 1993. Theories of Price Formation and Exchange in Double Oral Auctions. Working Paper 611, California Institute of Technology. URL http://EconPapers.repec.org/RePEc:clt:sswopa:611

Ellul, A., Shin, H. S., Tonks, I., et al., 2005. Opening and closing the market: Evidence from the London Stock Exchange. Journal of Financial and Quantitative Analysis 40 (4), 779.

Ferri, G., and Morone A., 2014. The effect of rating agencies on herd behavior. Journal of Economic Interaction and Coordination 9.1: 107-127.

Friedman, D., 1984. On the efficiency of experimental double auction markets. American Economic Review 74 (1), 60-72.

Friedman, D., 1991. A simple testable model of double auction markets. Journal of Economic Behavior and Organization 15 (1), 47-70.

Friedman, D., 1993. How trading institutions affect financial market performance: some laboratory evidence. Economic Inquiry 31 (3), 410-435.

Forsythe, R., Palfrey, T.R., Plott, C. R., 1982. Asset valuation in an experimental market. Econometrica 50 (3), 537-567.

Forsythe, R., and Lundholm, R., 1990. Information aggregation in an experimental market. Econometrica: Journal of the Econometric Society, 309-347.

Galton, F., 1907. Vox populi (the wisdom of crowds). Nature, 75(7), pp.450-451.

Gilovich, T., D. Griffin, D.Kahneman, 2002. Heuristics and Biases: The Psychology of Intuitive Judgment. Cambridge: Cambridge University Press.

Glosten, L.R., 1994. Is the electronic open limit order book inevitable? Journal of Finance 49 (4), 1127-1161.

Gode, Dhananjay and Shyam Sunder, 1991. Allocative efficiency of markets with zero intelligence (ZI) traders: Market as a partial substitute for individual rationality, Working paper no. 1992-16 (Carnegie Mellon Graduate School of Industrial Administration, Pittsburgh, PA.

Grossman, S., 1976. On the efficiency of competitive stock markets where trades have diverse information. The Journal of finance, 31(2), 573-585.

Grossman, S. J., and Stiglitz, J. E., 1980. On the impossibility of informationally efficient markets. The American economic review, 70(3), 393-408.

Hakenes, H., Schlegel, F., 2014. Exploiting the Financial Wisdom of the Crowd -- Crowdfunding as a Tool to Aggregate Vague Information. Available at SSRN: http://ssrn.com/abstract=2475025 or http://dx.doi.org/10.2139/ssrn.2475025

Heminway, J. M., 2013. Investor and Market Protection in the Crowdfunding Era: Disclosing to and for the Crowd. Vt. L. Rev., 38, 827.

Herzog, S.M. and Hertwig, R., 2011. The wisdom of ignorant crowds: Predicting sport outcomes by mere recognition. Judgment and Decision Making, 6(1), p.58.

Hirshleifer, D., and Shumway, T., 2003. Good da y sunshine: Stock returns and the weather. The Journal of Finance, 58 (3), 1009-1032.

Ho, T. S., Schwartz, R. A., Whitecomb, D. K., 1985. The trading decision and market clearing under transaction price uncertainty. Journal of Finance 40 (1), 21-42.

Holt, C. A., Porzio, M., Song, M., 2015. Price Bubbles, Expectations, and Gender in Asset Markets: An Experiment. University of Virginia Working Paper, june 26, 2015.

Hora, S. C., Fransen, B. R., Hawkins, N., and Susel, I., 2013. Median aggregation of distribution functions. Decision Analysis, 10(4), 279-291.

Huber, J., Kirchler, M., 2003. The value of information in markets with heterogeneously informed traders? a simulation and an experimental approach - different information

Huber, J., Kirchler, M. and Sutter, M., 2008. Is more information always better?: Experimental financial markets with cumulative information. Journal of Economic Behavior & Organization, 65(1), pp.86-104.

Huber, J., Kirchler, M., and Stefan, M., 2014. Experimental evidence on varying uncertainty and skewness in laboratory double auction markets

Hogarth, R.M., 1978. A note on aggregating opinions. Organizational Behavior and Human Performance, 21(1), pp.40-46.

Kalay, A., Wei, L., Wohl, A., 2002. Continuous trading or call auctions: Revealed preferences of investors at the Tel Aviv Stock Exchange. Journal of Finance 57 (1), 523-542.

Ketcham, J., Smith, V. L., Williams, A. W., 1984. A comparison of posted-offer and double-auction pricing institutions. Review of Economic Studies 51 (4), 595-614.

Kirchler, M., 2010. Partial knowledge is a dangerous thing? On the value of asymmetric fundamental information in asset markets. Journal of Economic Psychology, 31(4), 643-658.

Kirchler, M., and Huber, J., 2007. Fat tails and volatility clustering in experimental asset markets. Journal of Economic Dynamics and Control, 31(6), 1844-1874.

Kittur, A., Chi, E., Pendleton, B.A., Suh, B. and Mytkowicz, T., 2007. Power of the few vs. wisdom of the crowd: Wikipedia and the rise of the bourgeoisie. World wide web, 1(2), p.19.

Kuo, W., Li, Y.-C., 2011. Trading mechanisms and market quality: Call markets versus continuous auction markets. International Review of Finance 11 (4), 417-444.

Larrick, R.P., Mannes, A.E., Soll, J.B. and Krueger, J.I., 2011. The social psychology of the wisdom of crowds.

Lee, M.D., Zhang, S. and Shi, J., 2011. The wisdom of the crowd playing The Price Is Right. Memory \& cognition, 39(5), 914-923.

Lichtendahl Jr, K.C., Grushka-Cockayne, Y. and Pfeifer, P.E., 2013. The wisdom of competitive crowds. Operations Research, 61(6), 1383-1398.

Lorenz, J., Rauhut, H., Schweitzer, F. and Helbing, D., 2011. How social influence can undermine the wisdom of crowd effect. Proceedings of the National Academy of Sciences, 108(22), 9020-9025.

Makridakis, S., R.L. Winkler, 1983. Averages of forecasts: Some empirical results. Management Science 29 (9) 987-996.

Malone, T.W., Laubacher, R. and Dellarocas, C., 2009. Harnessing crowds: Mapping the genome of collective intelligence.

Martin, T. A., 2012. The JOBS act of 2012: Balancing fundamental securities law principles with the demands of the crowd.

Mendelson, H., 1982. Market behavior in a clearing house. Econometrica 50 (6), 1505-1524.

Mestelman, S., and Welland, D., 1992. Inventory carryover, experience, and clearance sales: a comparison of posted offer and double auction trading institutions. working paper, McMaster University.

Mollick, E., 2014. The dynamics of crowdfunding: An exploratory study. Journal of business venturing, 29(1), 1-16.

Morone, A., 2008. Financial markets in the laboratory: an experimental analysis of some stylized facts. Quantitative Finance, 8 (5), 513-532.

Morone, A., Nuzzo, S., Apr. 2016. Asset Markets in the Lab: a literature review. MPRA Paper 70461, University Library of Munich, Germany. URL https://ideas.repec.org/p/pra/mprapa/70461.html

Niederer, S. and Van Dijck, J., 2010. Wisdom of the crowd or technicity of content? Wikipedia as a sociotechnical system. New Media & Society, 12(8), 1368-1387.

O'brien, J., and Srivastava, S., 1991. Dynamic stock markets with multiple assets: An experimental analysis. The Journal of Finance, 46(5), 1811-1838.

Ockenfels, A., and Roth, A. E., 2006. Late and multiple bidding in second price Internet auctions: Theory and evidence concerning different rules for ending an auction. Games and Economic behavior, 55(2), 297-320.

Pagano, M. S., Peng, L., Schwartz, R. A., 2013. A call auction's impact on price formation and order routing: Evidence from the NASDAQ stock market. Journal of Financial Markets 16 (2), 331-261.

Plott, C. R., Smith, V. L.., 1978. An experimental examination of two exchange institutions. Review of Economic studies 45 (1), 133-153.

Plott, C.R. and Sunder, S., 1982. Efficiency of experimental security markets with insider information: An application of rational-expectations models. The Journal of Political Economy, 663-698.

Plott, C. R., and Sunder, S., 1988. Rational expectations and the aggregation of diverse information in laboratory security markets. Econometrica: Journal of the Econometric Society, 1085-1118.

Plott, C. R., 2000. Markets as information gathering tools. Southern Economic Journal, 67(1), 2-15.

Roll, R., 1988. The international crash of October 1987. Financial Analysts Journal 44(5), 19-35.

Rustichini, A., Satterthwaite, M. A., Williams, S. R., 1994. Convergence to efficiency in a simple market with incomplete information. Econometrica 62 (5), 1041-1063.

Satterthwaite, M. A., Williams, S. R., 1993. The Bayesian theory of the k-double auction. The Double Auction Market: Institutions, Theories and Evidence, 99-123.

Schnitzlein, C. R., 1996. Call and continuous trading mechanisms under asymetric information: An experimental investigation. Journal of Finance 51 (2), 613-636.

Schredelseker, K., 1984. Anlagestrategie und Informationsnutzen am Aktienmarkt. Zeitschrift für betriebswirtschaftliche Forschung, 36, 44-59.

Smith,V. L., 1962. An experimental study of competitive market behavior. Journal of Political Economy 70 (2), 111-137.

Smith, V. L., 1964. Effect of market organization on competitive equilibrium. Quarterly Journal of Economics 78 (2), 182-201.

Smith, J. W., 2007. Nasdaqs electronic closing cross: An empirical analysis. In: The New Nasdaq Marketplace. Springer, 103-132.

Smith, V. L., Willians, A.W., Bratton, W. K., Vannoni, M. G., 1982. Competitive market institutions: Double auctions vs. sealed bid-offer auctions. American Economic Review 72 (1), 58-77.

Smith, J. W., 2007. Nasdaqs electronic closing cross: An empirical analysis. In: The New Nasdaq Marketplace. Springer, 103-132.

Soll, J.B., R. P. Larrick., 2009. Strategies for revising judgment: how (and how well) people use other opinions, Journal of Experimental Psychology: Learning, Memory and Cognition 35 (3) 780-805.

Sunder, S., 1992. Experimental asset markets: A survey. Carnegie Mellon University.

Sunder, S., 1995. Experimental Asset Markets: A Survey. In: Kagel, J.H., Roth, A. E. (Eds.), Handbook of Experimental Economics. Princton University Press, 445-500.

Surowiecki, J., 2004. The wisdom of crowds: why the many are smarter than the few and how collective wisdom shapes business, economics, society and nations. Little, Brown.

Theissen, E., 2000. Market structure, informational efficiency and liquidity: An experimental comparison of auction and dealer markets. Journal of Financial Markets 3 (4), 333-363.

Wikipedia, USS Scorpion; Date: 01.05.2017, 10:00; https://de.wikipedia.org/wiki/USS_Scorpion_(SSN-589)

Wilson, R. B., 1987. Arrow and the Ascent of Modern Economic Theory. Palgrave Macmillan UK, London, Ch. On Equilibria of Bid-Ask Markets, 375-414.

MIX
Papier aus verantwortungsvollen Quellen
Paper from responsible sources
FSC® C105338

If you have any concerns about our products,
you can contact us on
ProductSafety@springernature.com

In case Publisher is established outside the EU,
the EU authorized representative is:
Springer Nature Customer Service Center GmbH
Europaplatz 3, 69115 Heidelberg, Germany

Printed by Libri Plureos GmbH
in Hamburg, Germany